(COVER
NOT
FINAL)

MAX HUFFMAN

ADHOUSE BOOKS
RICHMOND, VA

COVER NOT FINAL
CRIME FUNNIES
BY MAX HUFFMAN
PUBLISHED BY ADHOUSE BOOKS

ISBN 1-935233-65-3
ISBN 978-1-935233-65-7
10 9 8 7 6 5 4 3 2 1

DESIGN: HUFFMAN + PITZER

ADHOUSE BOOKS
3905 BROOK ROAD
RICHMOND, VA 23227 USA
www.adhousebooks.com

FIRST PRINTING, JUNE 2021

PRINTED IN CANADA

IN THIS ISSUE:

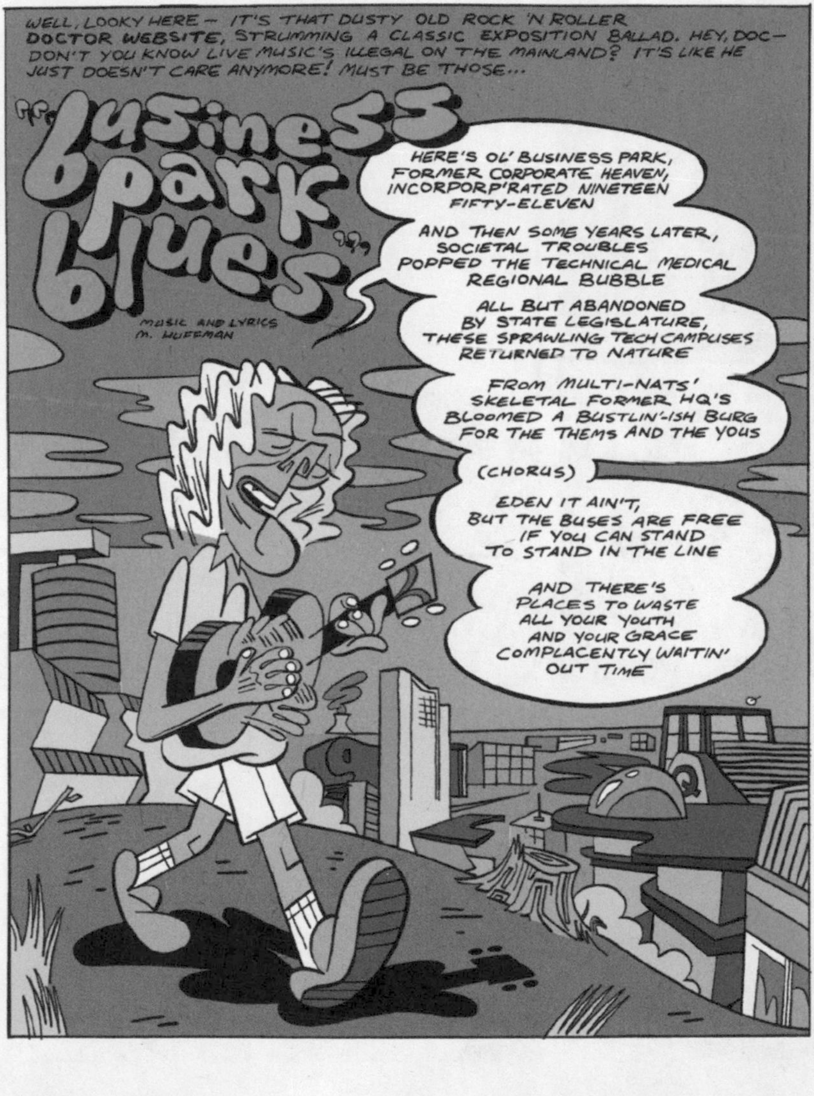
WELL, LOOKY HERE — IT'S THAT DUSTY OLD ROCK 'N ROLLER DOCTOR WEBSITE, STRUMMING A CLASSIC EXPOSITION BALLAD. HEY, DOC— DON'T YOU KNOW LIVE MUSIC'S ILLEGAL ON THE MAINLAND? IT'S LIKE HE JUST DOESN'T CARE ANYMORE! MUST BE THOSE...
"business park blues"
MUSIC AND LYRICS M. HUFFMAN
HERE'S OL' BUSINESS PARK, FORMER CORPORATE HEAVEN, INCORPORP'RATED NINETEEN FIFTY-ELEVEN
AND THEN SOME YEARS LATER, SOCIETAL TROUBLES POPPED THE TECHNICAL MEDICAL REGIONAL BUBBLE
ALL BUT ABANDONED BY STATE LEGISLATURE, THESE SPRAWLING TECH CAMPUSES RETURNED TO NATURE
FROM MULTI-NATS' SKELETAL FORMER HQ'S BLOOMED A BUSTLIN'-ISH BURG FOR THE THEMS AND THE YOUS
(CHORUS)
EDEN IT AIN'T, BUT THE BUSES ARE FREE IF YOU CAN STAND TO STAND IN THE LINE
AND THERE'S PLACES TO WASTE ALL YOUR YOUTH AND YOUR GRACE COMPLACENTLY WAITIN' OUT TIME

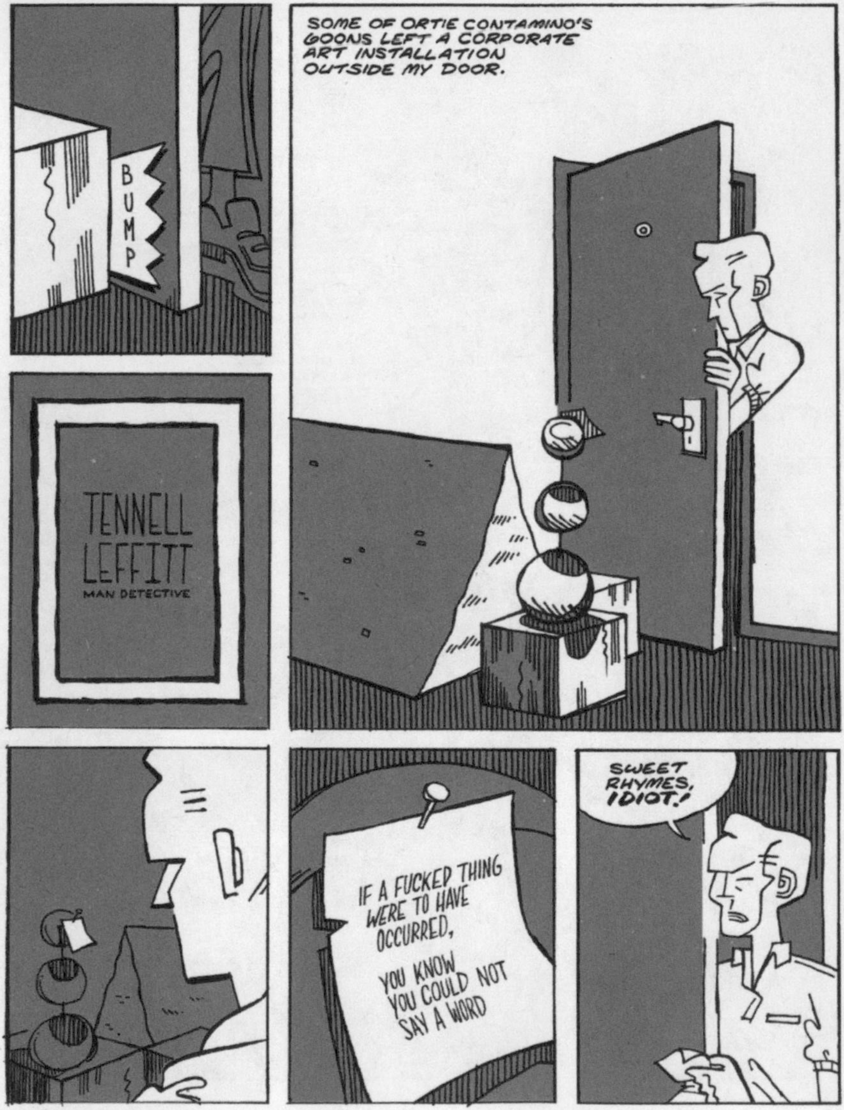
BUMP
TENNELL LEFFITT
MAN DETECTIVE
SOME OF ORTIE CONTAMINO'S GOONS LEFT A CORPORATE ART INSTALLATION OUTSIDE MY DOOR.
IF A FUCKED THING WERE TO HAVE OCCURRED,
YOU KNOW YOU COULD NOT SAY A WORD
SWEET RHYMES, IDIOT.!

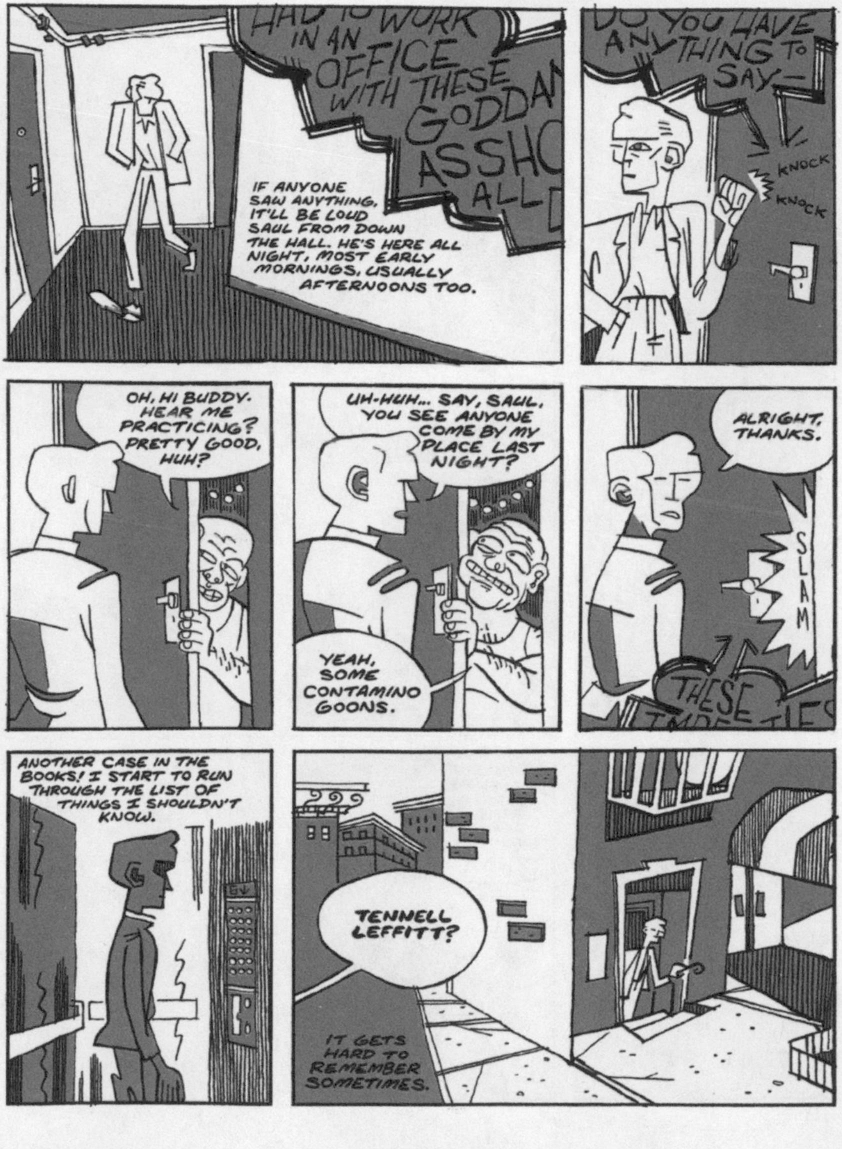
IN AN WORK
OFFICE
WITH THESE
GODDA
ASSHO
ALL
IF ANYONE SAW ANYTHING, IT'LL BE LOUD SAUL FROM DOWN THE HALL. HE'S HERE ALL NIGHT, MOST EARLY MORNINGS, USUALLY AFTERNOONS TOO.
YOU HAVE ANYTHING TO SAY—
KNOCK
KNOCK
OH, HI BUDDY. HEAR ME PRACTICING? PRETTY GOOD, HUH?
UH-HUH... SAY, SAUL, YOU SEE ANYONE COME BY MY PLACE LAST NIGHT?
YEAH, SOME CONTAMINO GOONS.
ALRIGHT, THANKS.
SLAM
THESE
ANOTHER CASE IN THE BOOKS! I START TO RUN THROUGH THE LIST OF THINGS I SHOULDN'T KNOW.
TENNELL LEFFITT?
IT GETS HARD TO REMEMBER SOMETIMES.

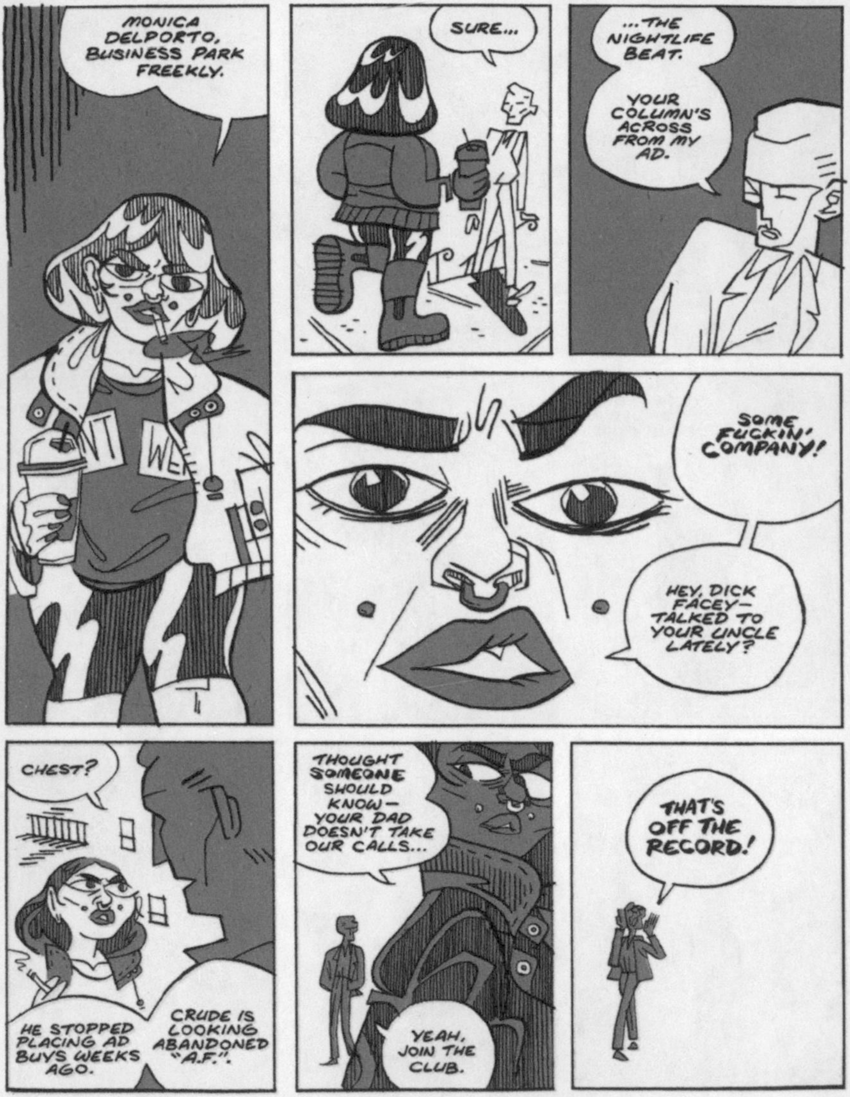
MONICA DELPORTO, BUSINESS PARK FREEKLY.
SURE...
...THE NIGHTLIFE BEAT.
YOUR COLUMN'S ACROSS FROM MY AD.
SOME FUCKIN' COMPANY!
HEY, DICK FACEY— TALKED TO YOUR UNCLE LATELY?
CHEST?
HE STOPPED PLACING AD BUYS WEEKS AGO.
CRUDE IS LOOKING ABANDONED "A.F.".
THOUGHT SOMEONE SHOULD KNOW— YOUR DAD DOESN'T TAKE OUR CALLS...
YEAH. JOIN THE CLUB.
THAT'S OFF THE RECORD!

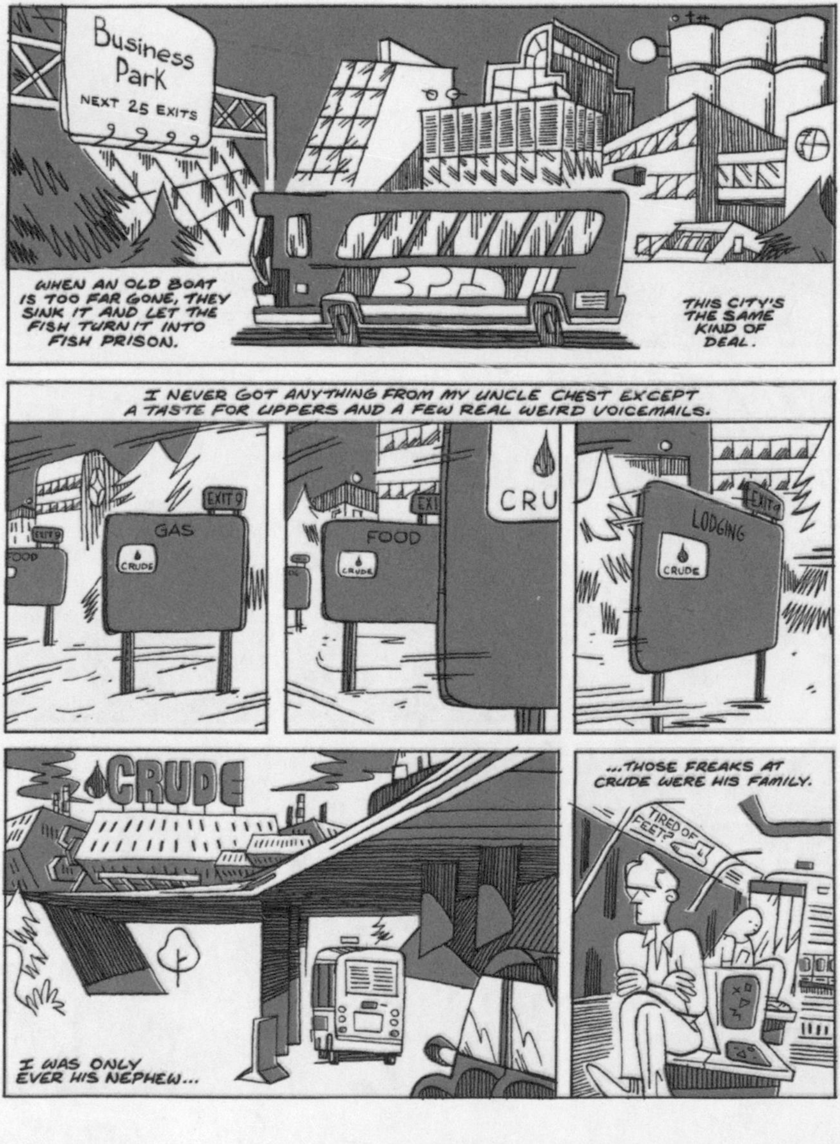
Business Park
NEXT 25 EXITS
WHEN AN OLD BOAT IS TOO FAR GONE, THEY SINK IT AND LET THE FISH TURN IT INTO FISH PRISON.
THIS CITY'S THE SAME KIND OF DEAL.
I NEVER GOT ANYTHING FROM MY UNCLE CHEST EXCEPT A TASTE FOR UPPERS AND A FEW REAL WEIRD VOICEMAILS.
EXIT 9
GAS
CRUDE
FOOD
CRU
LODGING
CRUDE
I WAS ONLY EVER HIS NEPHEW...
...THOSE FREAKS AT CRUDE WERE HIS FAMILY.
TIRED OF FEET?

I'M GETTING ONE OF MY CLASSIC DETECTIVE HUNCHES...

IT'S TELLING ME THIS PLACE IS A GHOST TOWN.

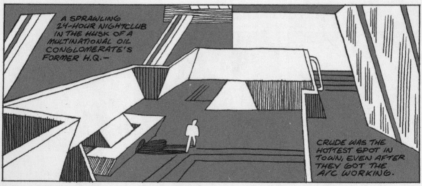

A SPRAWLING 24-HOUR NIGHTCLUB IN THE HUSK OF A MULTINATIONAL OIL CONGLOMERATE'S FORMER H.Q.—

CRUDE WAS THE HOTTEST SPOT IN TOWN, EVEN AFTER THEY GOT THE A/C WORKING.

IMPROPRIETOR

SO WHY'S IT GUTTED?

WHERE'S CHEST?

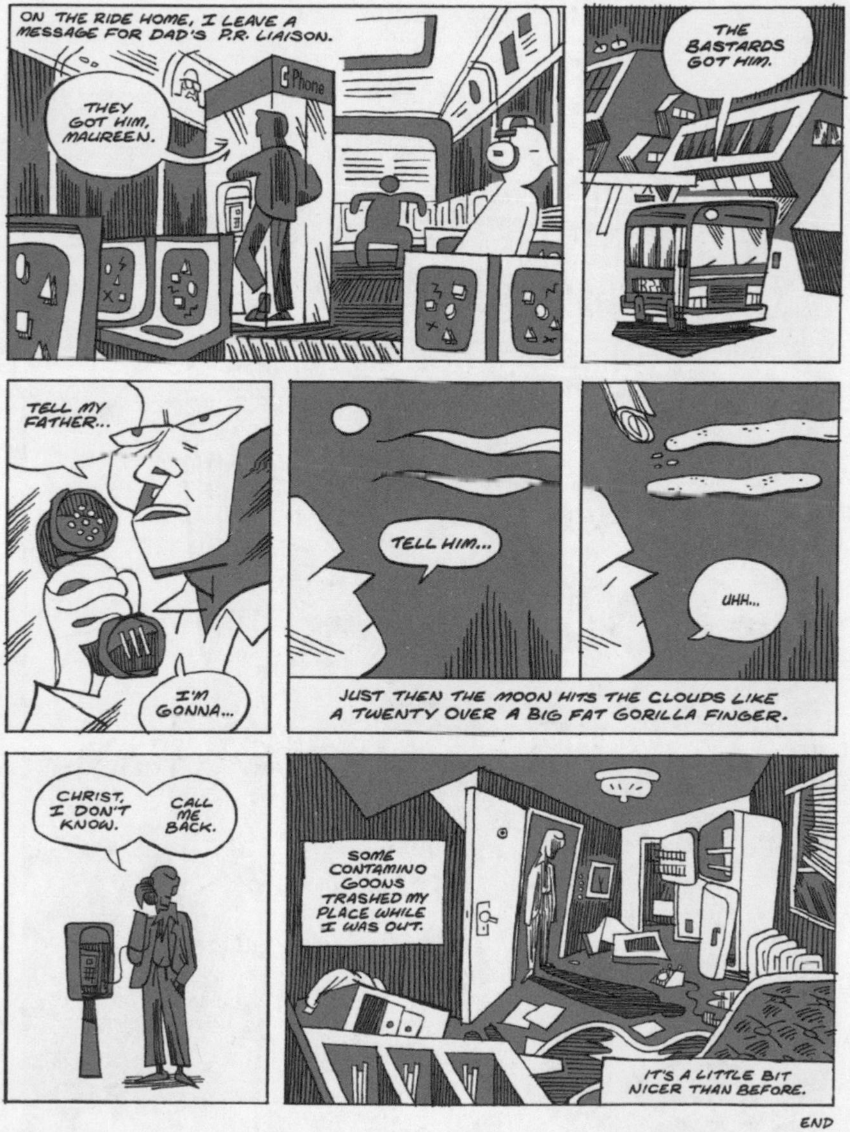
ON THE RIDE HOME, I LEAVE A MESSAGE FOR DAD'S P.R. LIAISON.
Phone
THEY GOT HIM, MAUREEN.
THE BASTARDS GOT HIM.
TELL MY FATHER...
I'M GONNA...
TELL HIM...
UHH...
JUST THEN THE MOON HITS THE CLOUDS LIKE A TWENTY OVER A BIG FAT GORILLA FINGER.
CHRIST, I DON'T KNOW.
CALL ME BACK.
SOME CONTAMINO GOONS TRASHED MY PLACE WHILE I WAS OUT.
IT'S A LITTLE BIT NICER THAN BEFORE.

END

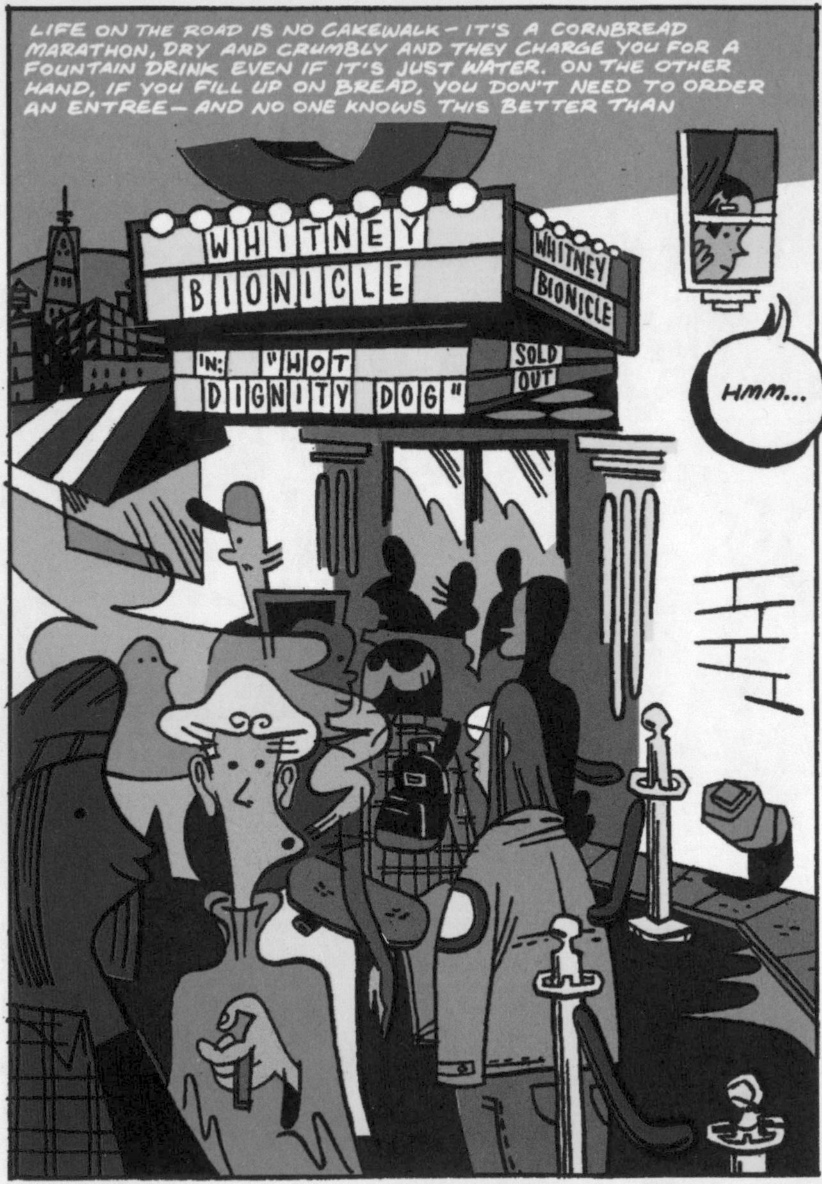
LIFE ON THE ROAD IS NO CAKEWALK – IT'S A CORNBREAD MARATHON, DRY AND CRUMBLY AND THEY CHARGE YOU FOR A FOUNTAIN DRINK EVEN IF IT'S JUST WATER. ON THE OTHER HAND, IF YOU FILL UP ON BREAD, YOU DON'T NEED TO ORDER AN ENTREE – AND NO ONE KNOWS THIS BETTER THAN
WHITNEY BIONICLE
WHITNEY BIONICLE
IN: "HOT DIGNITY DOG"
SOLD OUT
HMM...

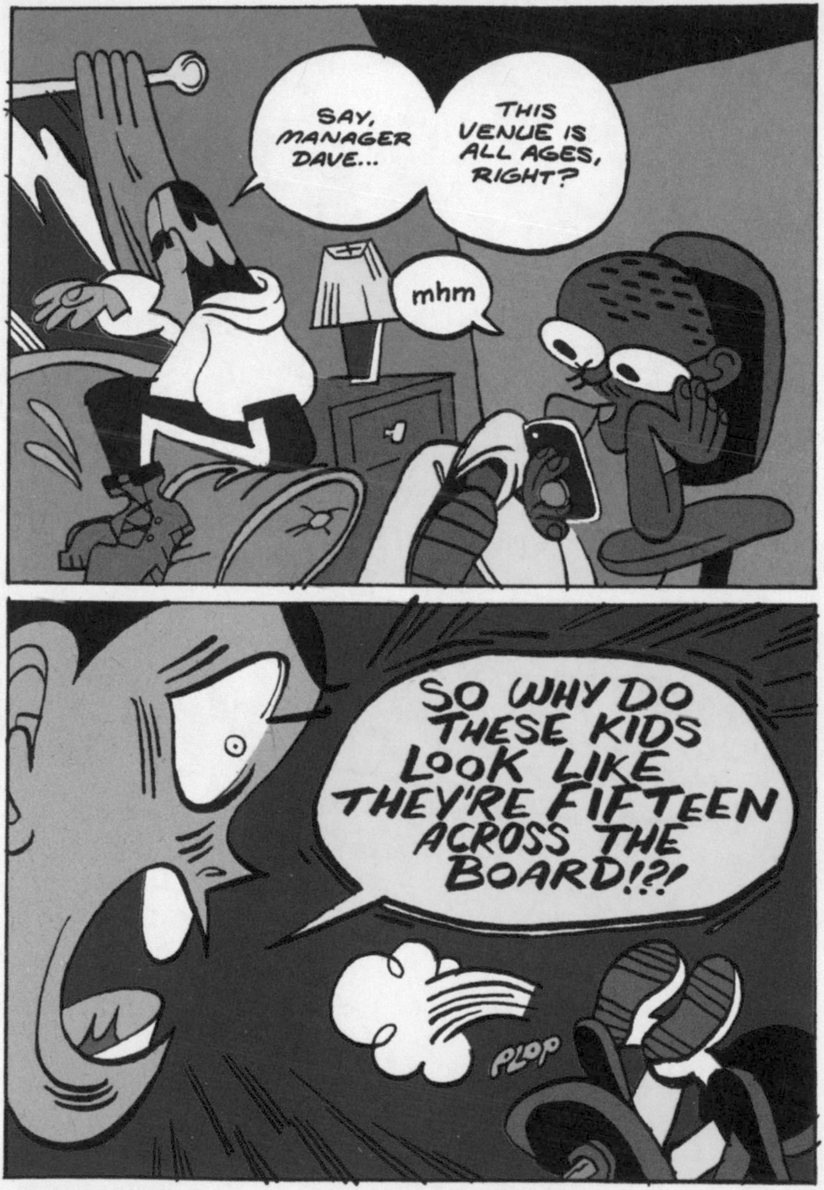
SAY, MANAGER DAVE...
THIS VENUE IS ALL AGES, RIGHT?
mhm
SO WHY DO THESE KIDS LOOK LIKE THEY'RE FIFTEEN ACROSS THE BOARD!?!
PLOP

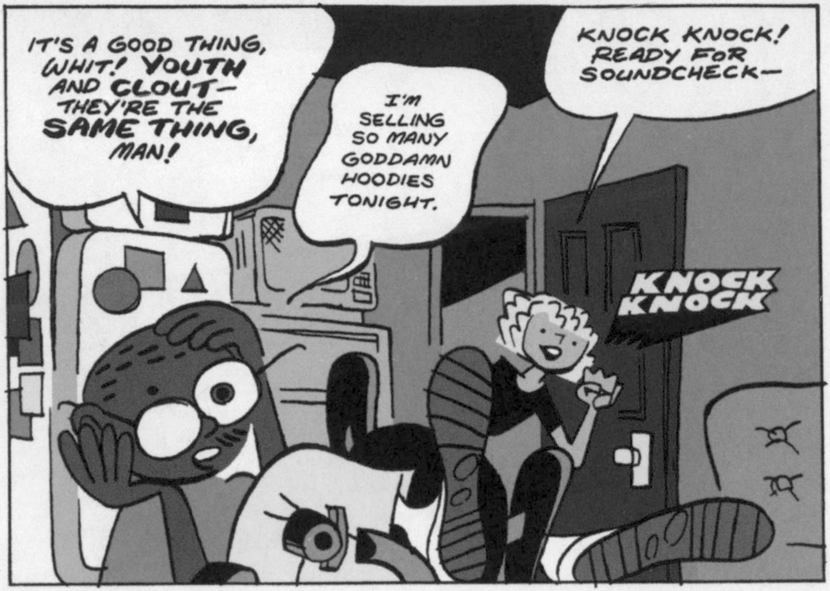
IT'S A GOOD THING, WHIT! YOUTH AND CLOUT— THEY'RE THE SAME THING, MAN!
I'M SELLING SO MANY GODDAMN HOODIES TONIGHT.
KNOCK KNOCK! READY FOR SOUNDCHECK—
KNOCK KNOCK
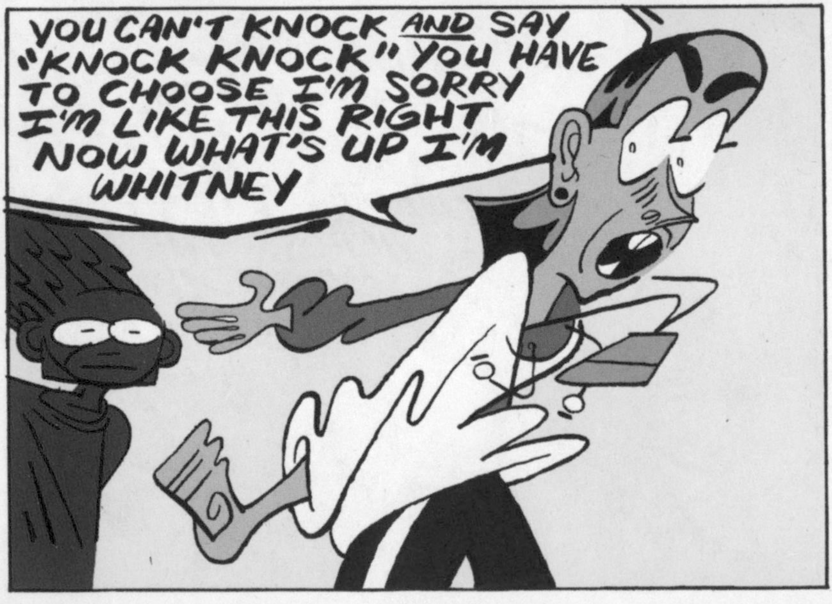
YOU CAN'T KNOCK AND SAY "KNOCK KNOCK" YOU HAVE TO CHOOSE I'M SORRY I'M LIKE THIS RIGHT NOW WHAT'S UP I'M WHITNEY

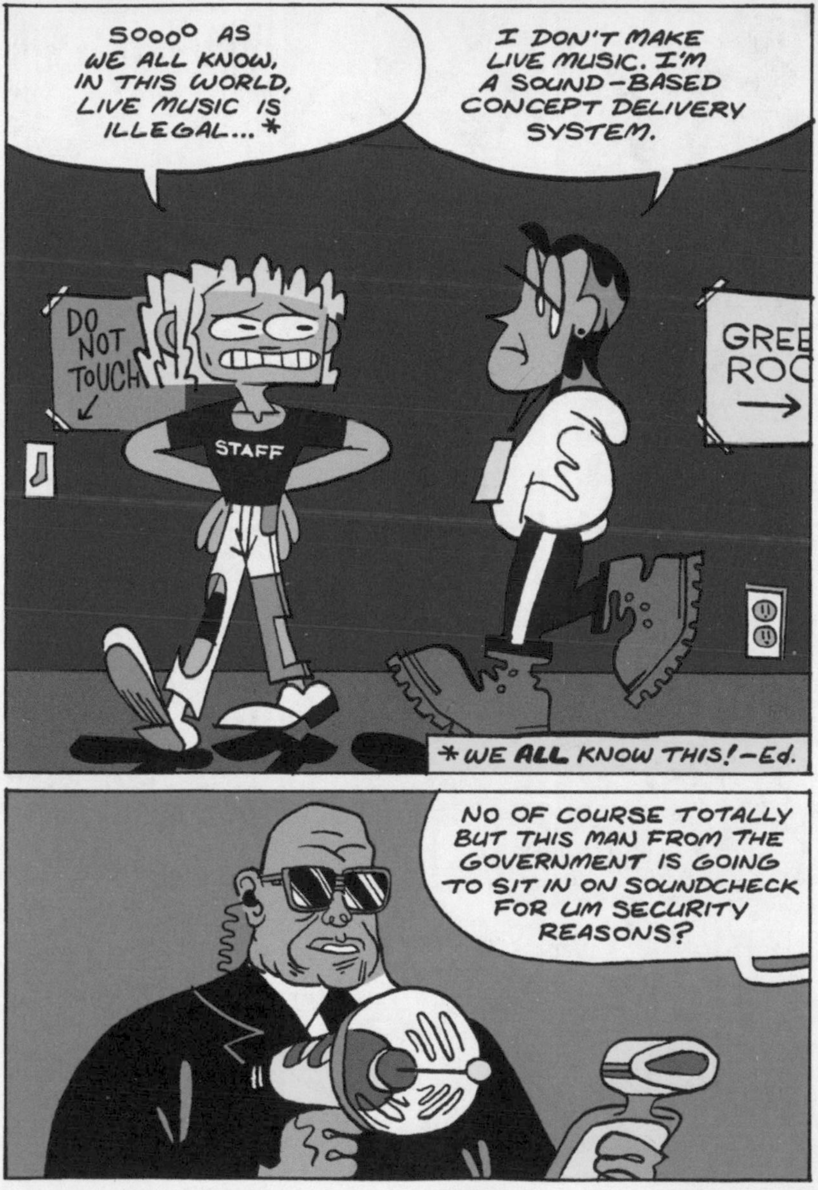
SOOOO AS WE ALL KNOW, IN THIS WORLD, LIVE MUSIC IS ILLEGAL...*
I DON'T MAKE LIVE MUSIC. I'M A SOUND-BASED CONCEPT DELIVERY SYSTEM.
DO NOT TOUCH
STAFF
*WE ALL KNOW THIS! —Ed.
NO OF COURSE TOTALLY BUT THIS MAN FROM THE GOVERNMENT IS GOING TO SIT IN ON SOUNDCHECK FOR UM SECURITY REASONS?

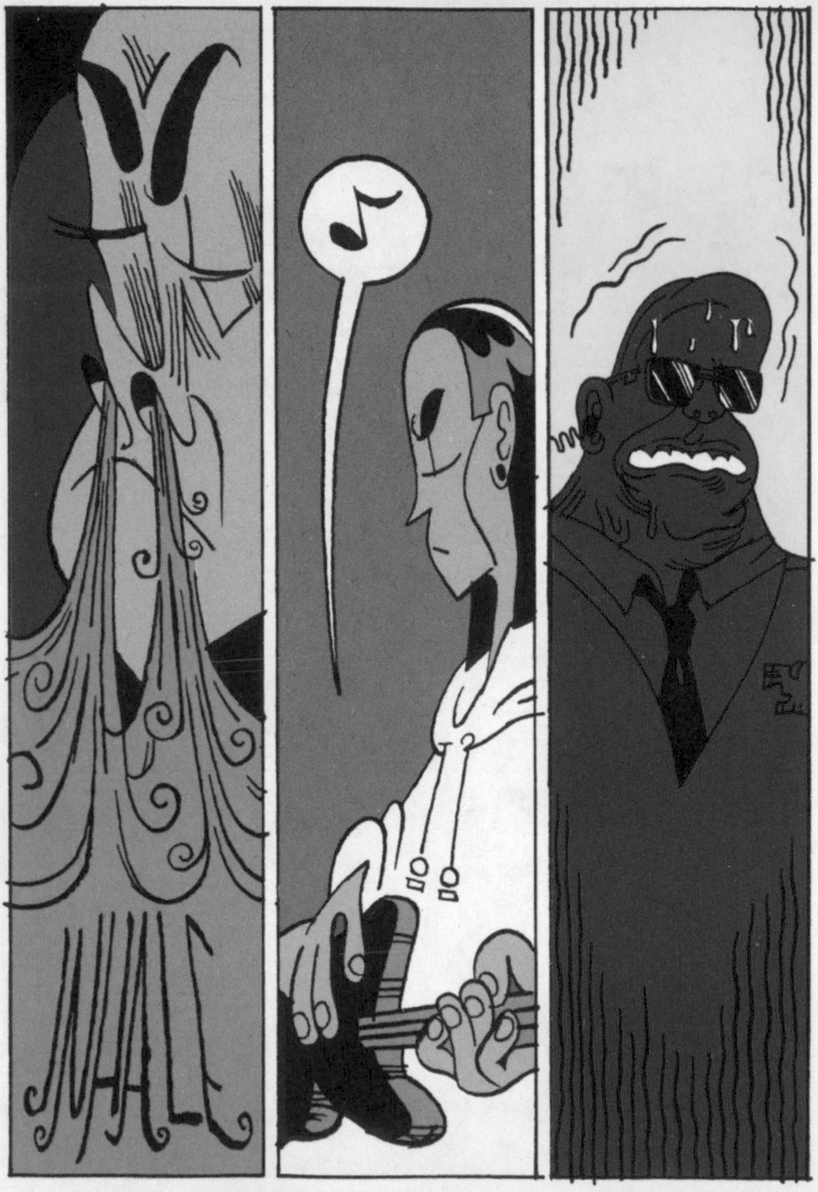

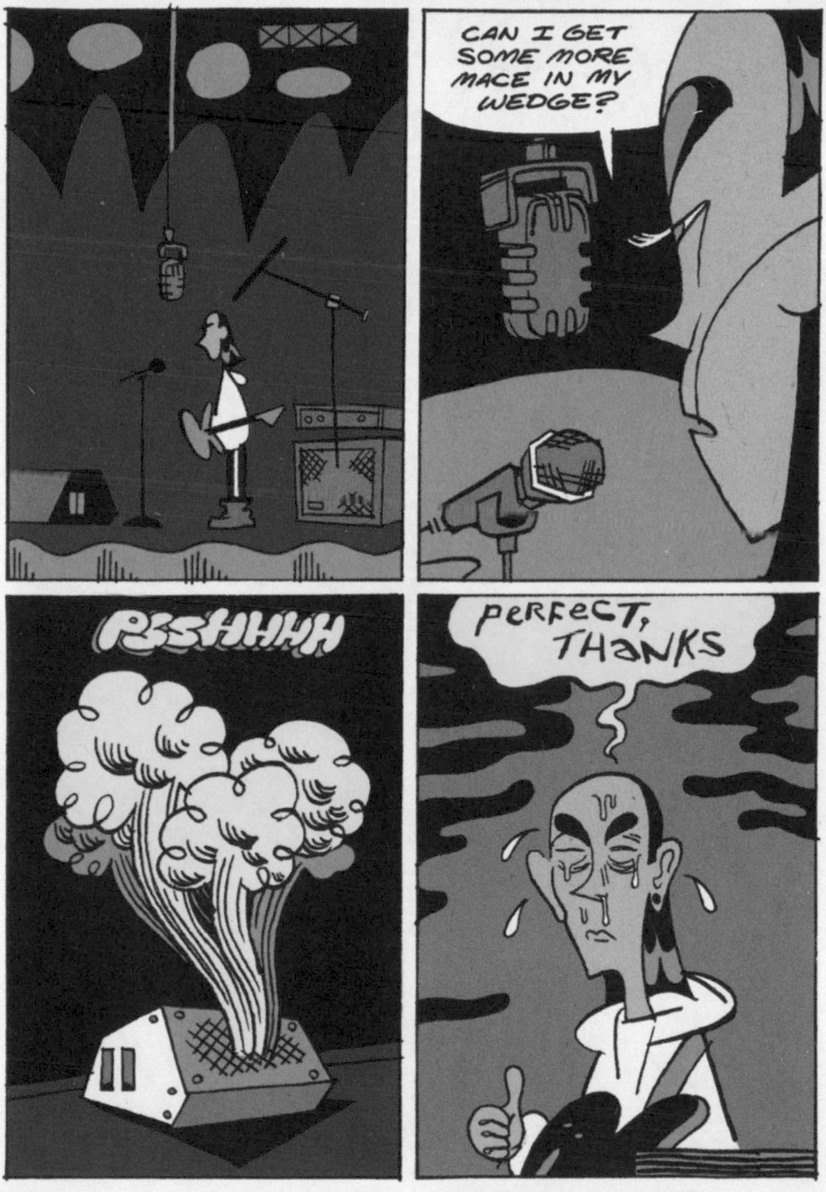
CAN I GET SOME MORE MACE IN MY WEDGE?
PFSSHHHH
PERFECT, THANKS

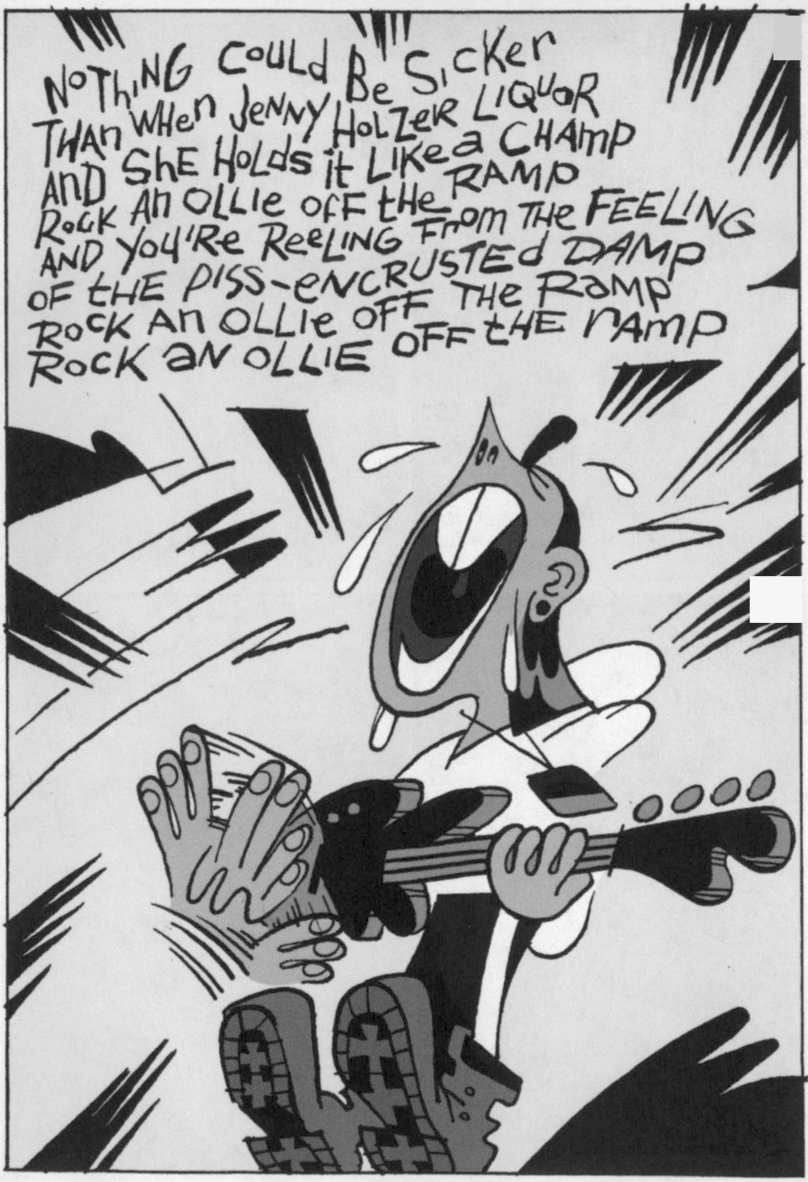

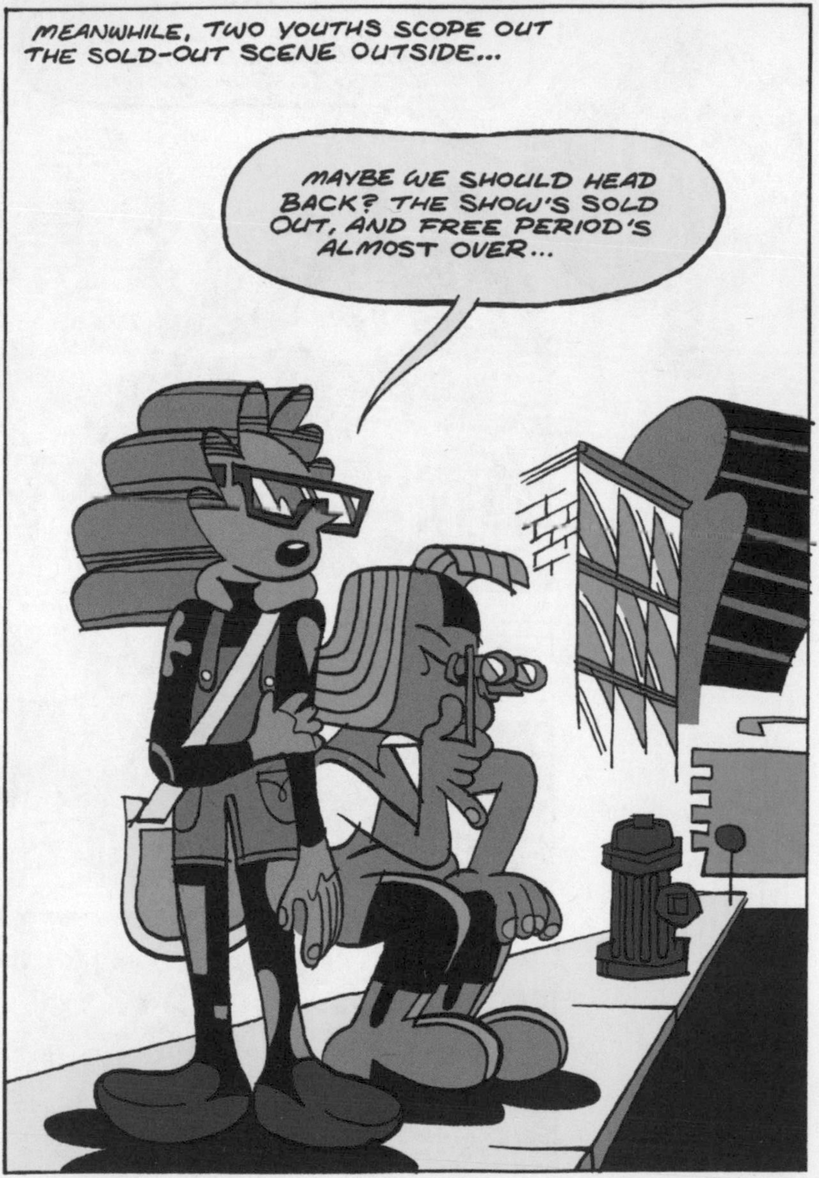
MEANWHILE, TWO YOUTHS SCOPE OUT THE SOLD-OUT SCENE OUTSIDE...
MAYBE WE SHOULD HEAD BACK? THE SHOW'S SOLD OUT, AND FREE PERIOD'S ALMOST OVER...

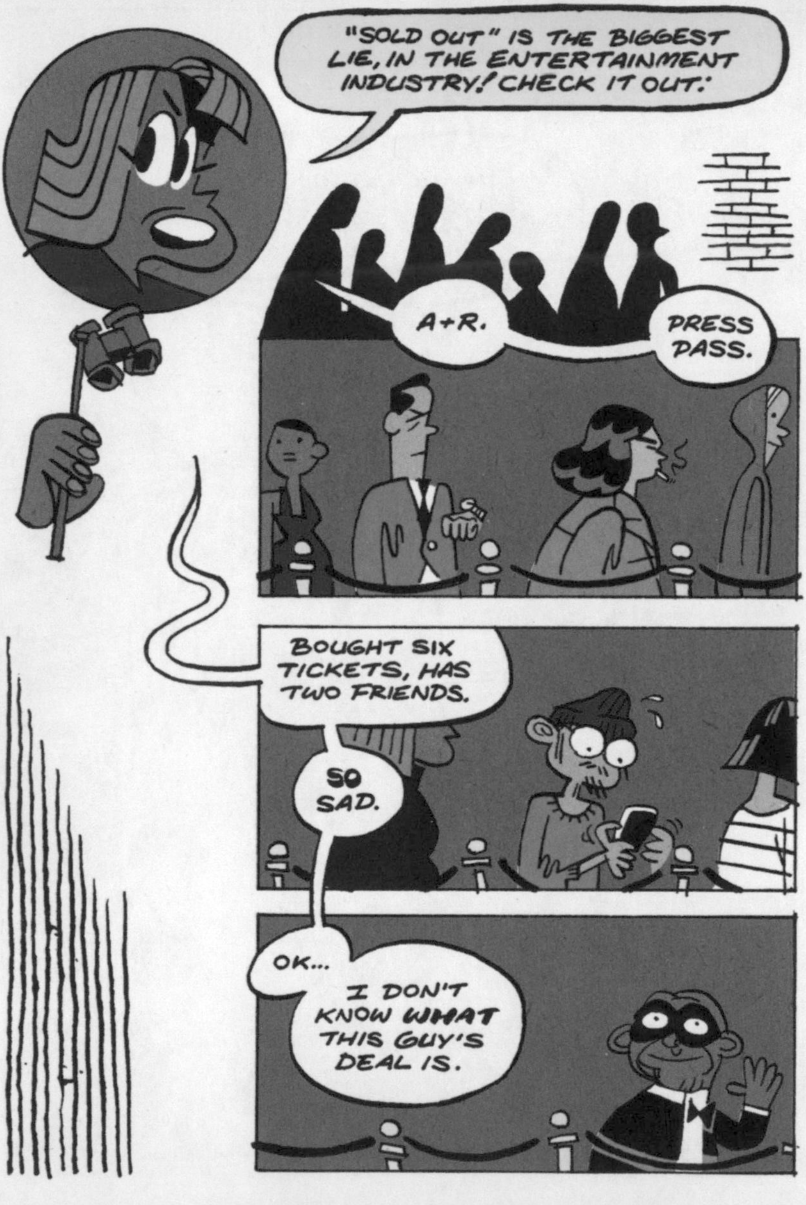
"SOLD OUT" IS THE BIGGEST LIE, IN THE ENTERTAINMENT INDUSTRY! CHECK IT OUT:
A+R.
PRESS PASS.
BOUGHT SIX TICKETS, HAS TWO FRIENDS.
SO SAD.
OK...
I DON'T KNOW WHAT THIS GUY'S DEAL IS.

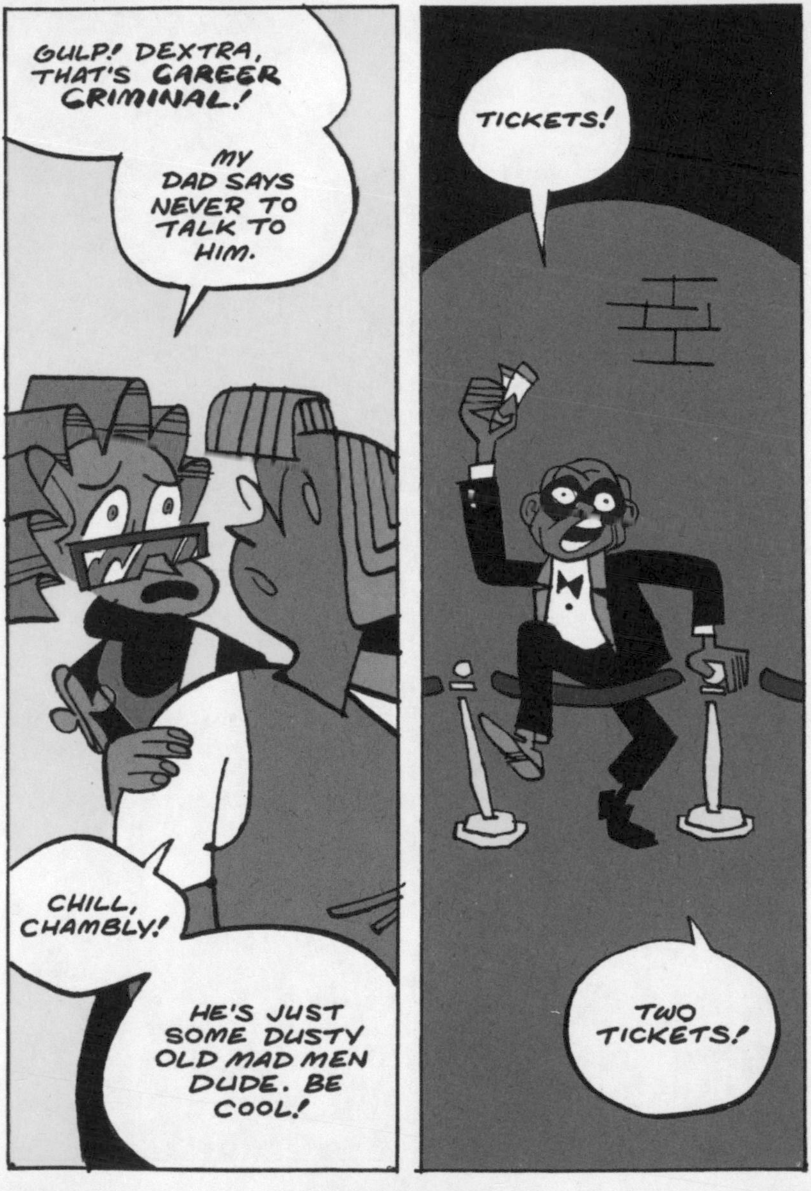
GULP! DEXTRA, THAT'S CAREER CRIMINAL!
MY DAD SAYS NEVER TO TALK TO HIM.
CHILL, CHAMBLY!
HE'S JUST SOME DUSTY OLD MAD MEN DUDE. BE COOL!
TICKETS!
TWO TICKETS!

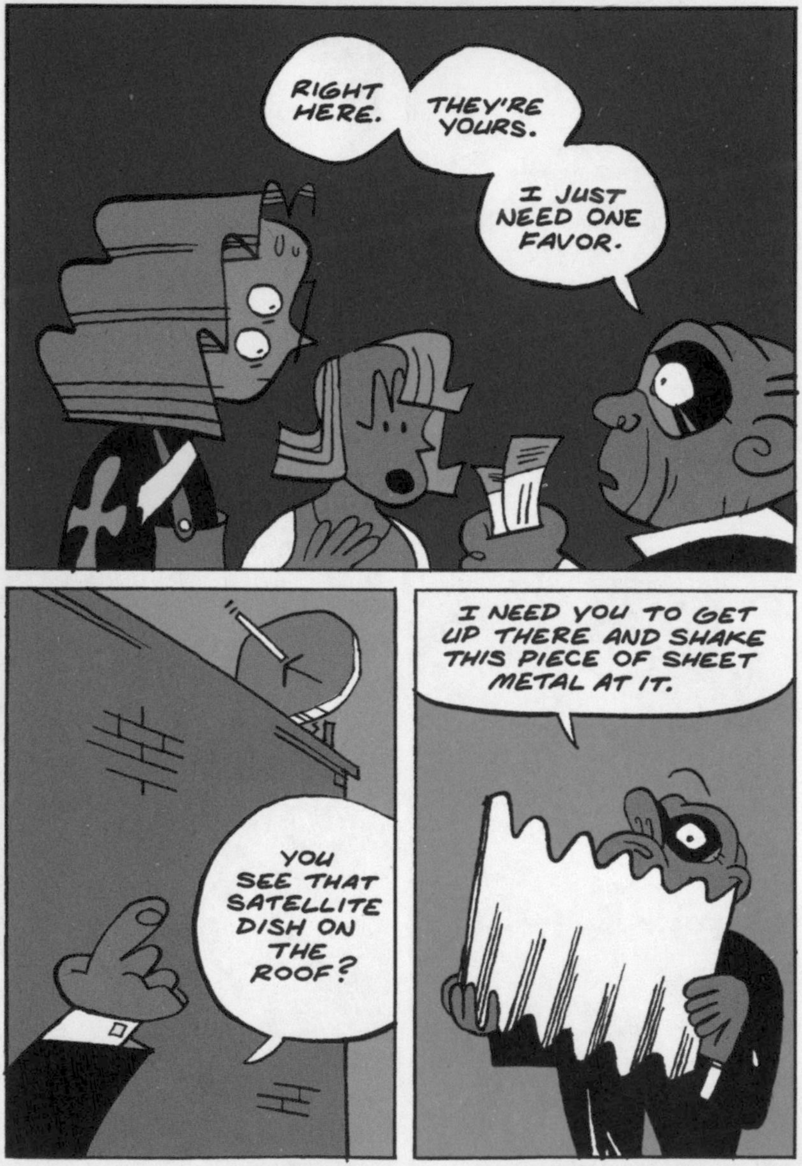
RIGHT HERE.
THEY'RE YOURS.
I JUST NEED ONE FAVOR.
YOU SEE THAT SATELLITE DISH ON THE ROOF?
I NEED YOU TO GET UP THERE AND SHAKE THIS PIECE OF SHEET METAL AT IT.

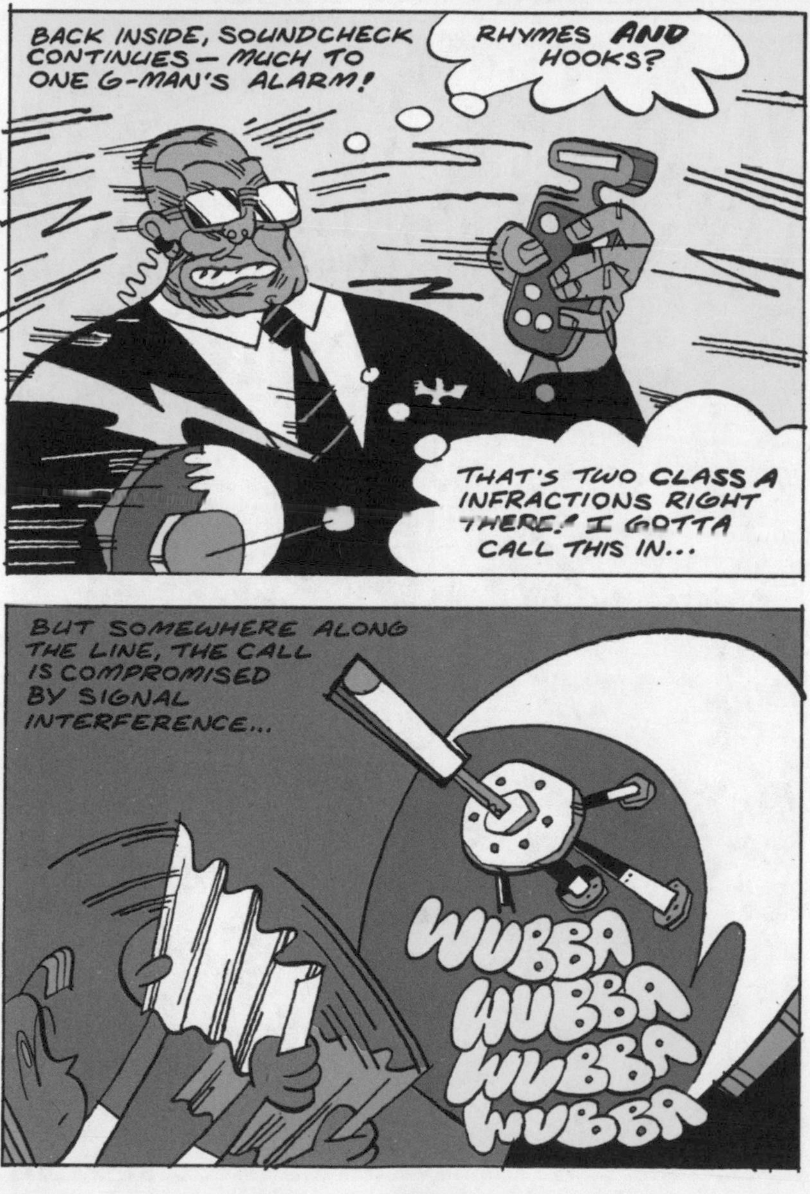
BACK INSIDE, SOUNDCHECK CONTINUES— MUCH TO ONE G-MAN'S ALARM!
RHYMES AND HOOKS?
THAT'S TWO CLASS A INFRACTIONS RIGHT THERE! I GOTTA CALL THIS IN...
BUT SOMEWHERE ALONG THE LINE, THE CALL IS COMPROMISED BY SIGNAL INTERFERENCE...
WUBBA WUBBA WUBBA WUBBA

...AND AT THE TONAL REGULATORY BODY HEADQUARTERS IN SECAUCUS, NJ...

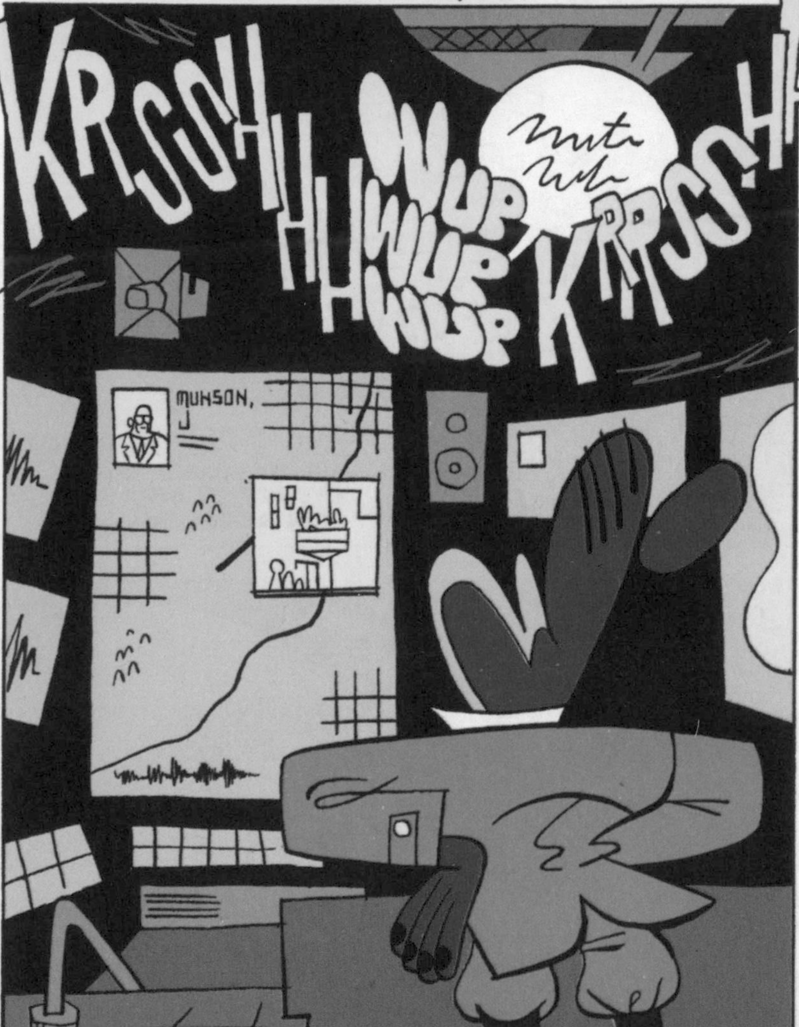
KRSCHHH
HWUP
HWUP
HWUP
KRRSCHHH
MUNSON, J

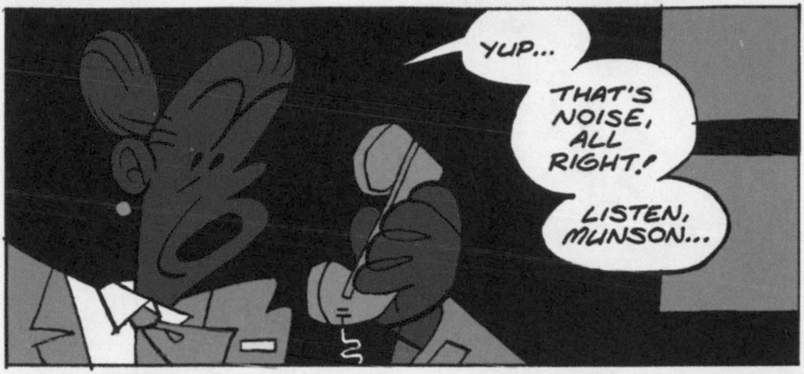
YUP...
THAT'S NOISE, ALL RIGHT!
LISTEN, MUNSON...

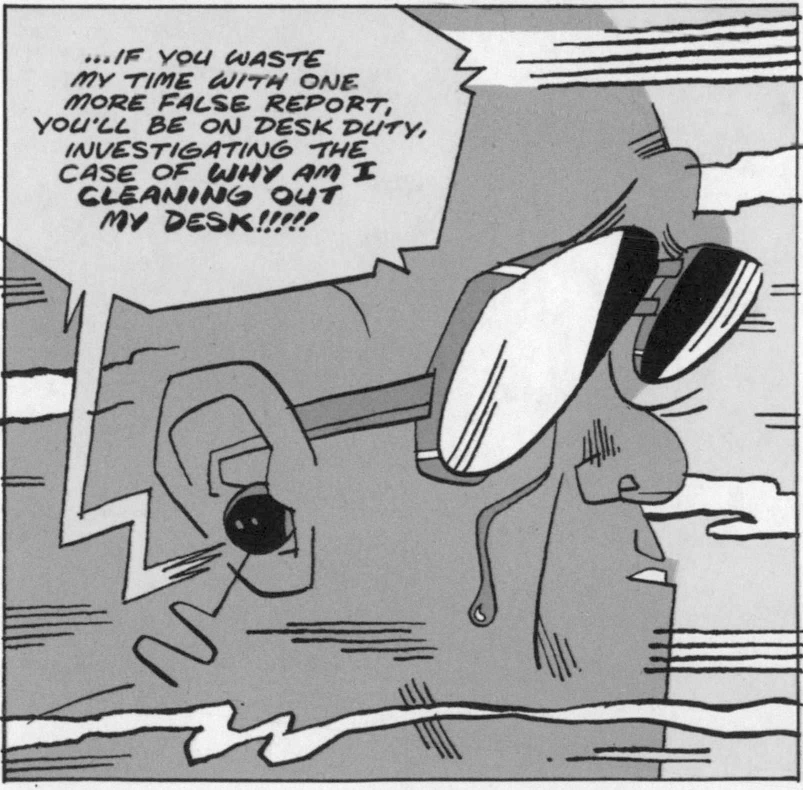
...IF YOU WASTE MY TIME WITH ONE MORE FALSE REPORT, YOU'LL BE ON DESK DUTY, INVESTIGATING THE CASE OF WHY AM I CLEANING OUT MY DESK!!!!!

AND SO, LATER:

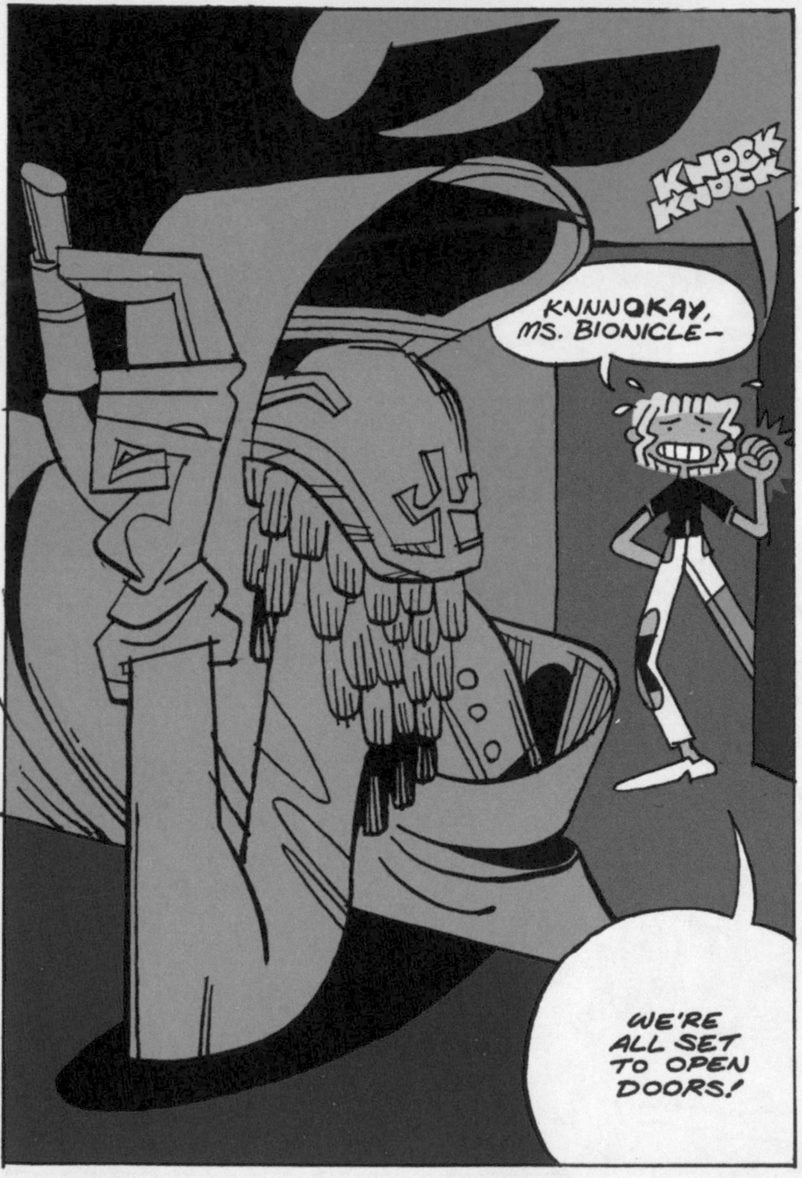
KNOCK KNOCK
KNNNOKAY, MS. BIONICLE-
WE'RE ALL SET TO OPEN DOORS!

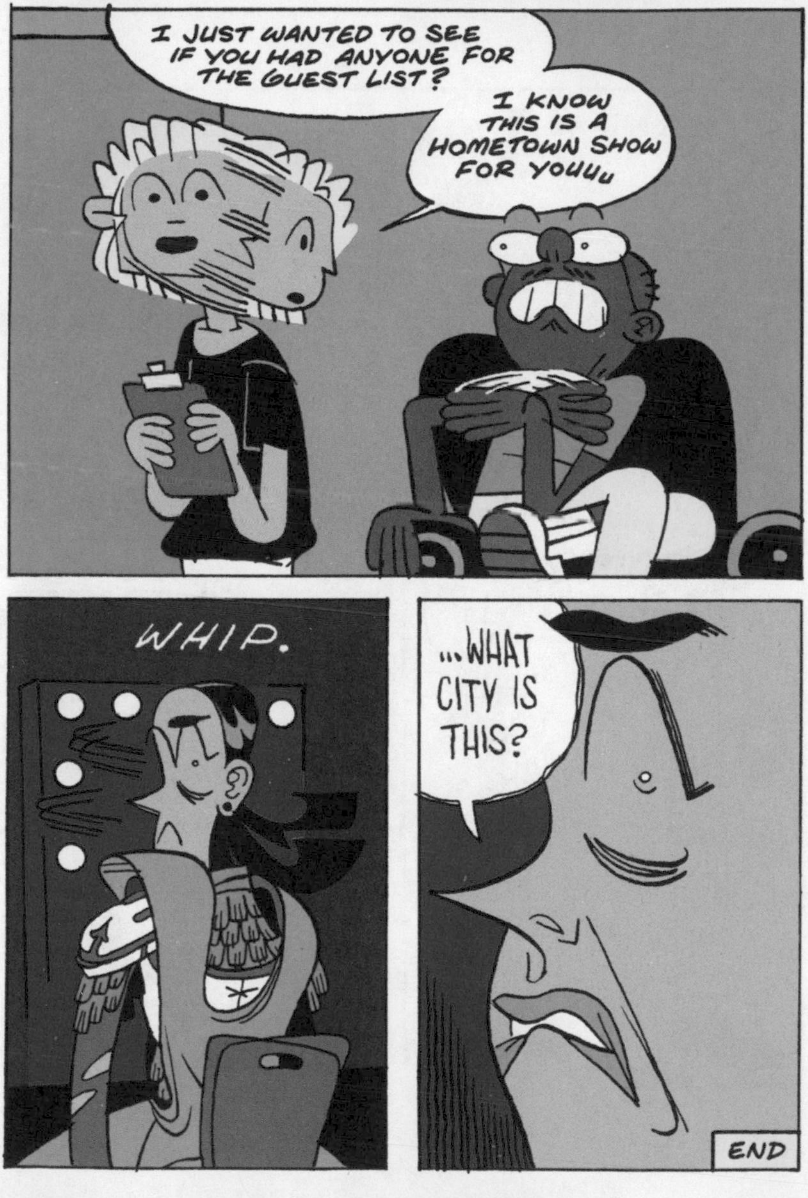

I JUST WANTED TO SEE IF YOU HAD ANYONE FOR THE GUEST LIST?
I KNOW THIS IS A HOMETOWN SHOW FOR YOUUU
WHIP.
...WHAT CITY IS THIS?
END

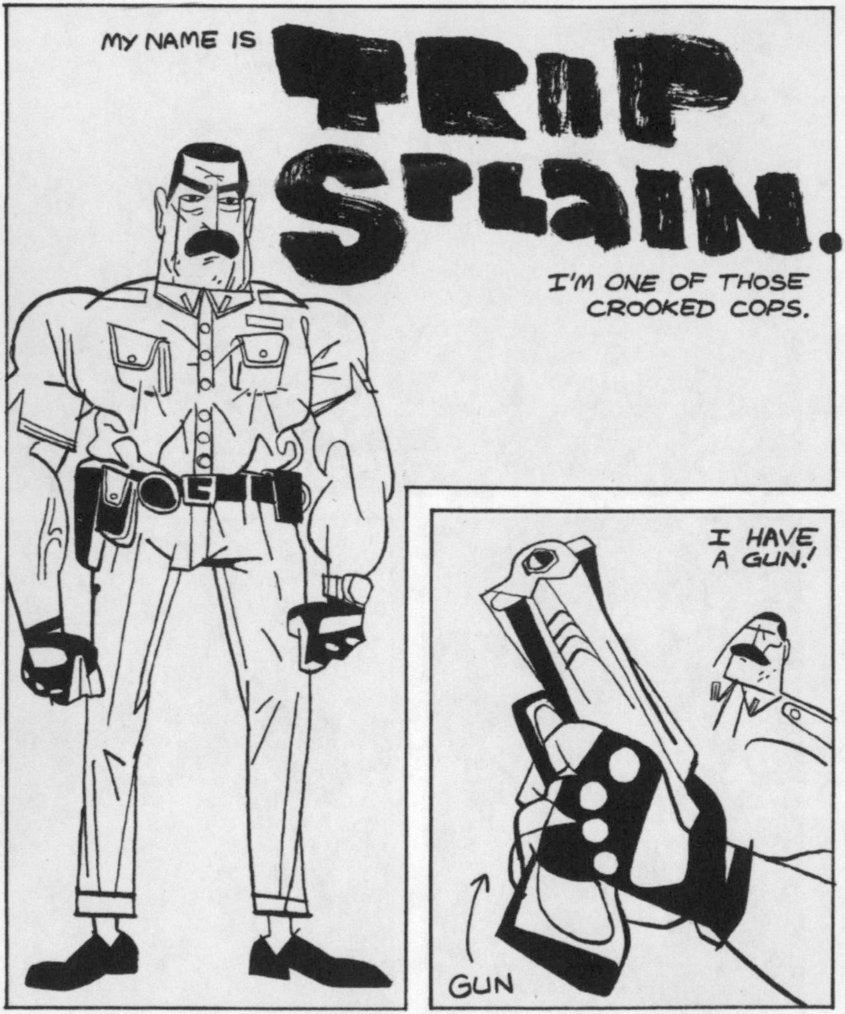
MY NAME IS
TRIP SPLAIN.
I'M ONE OF THOSE CROOKED COPS.
I HAVE A GUN!
GUN

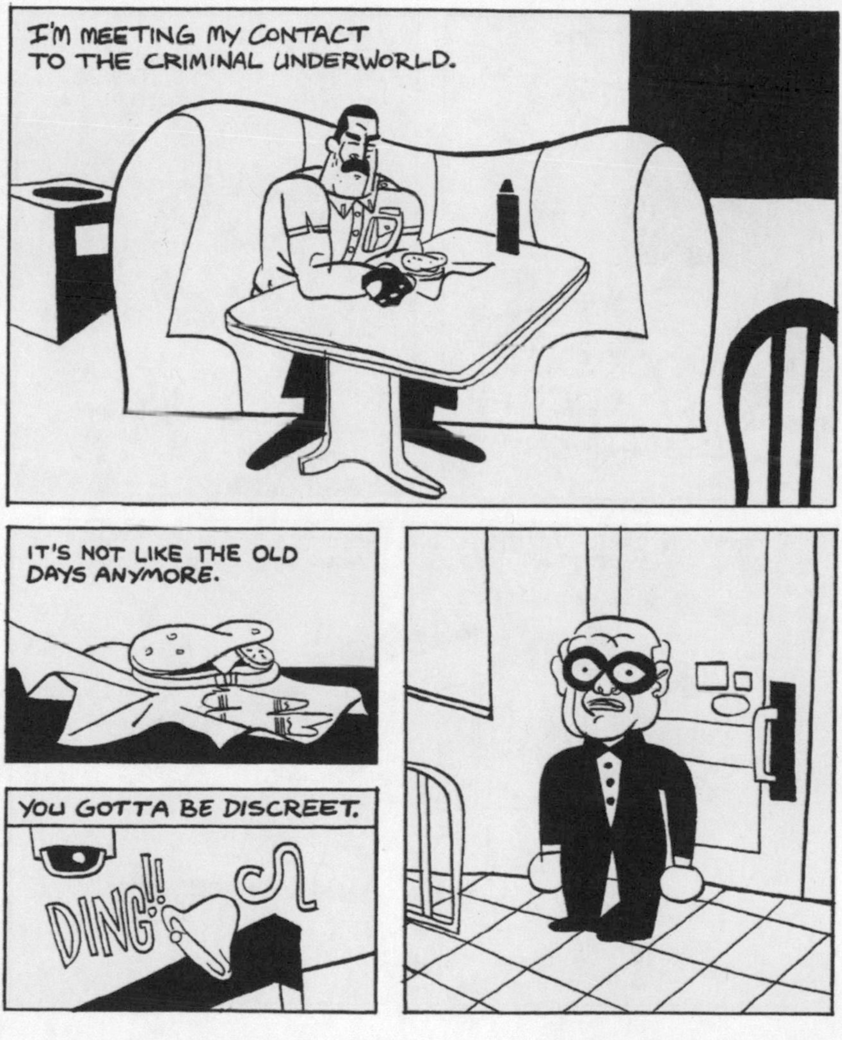
I'M MEETING MY CONTACT TO THE CRIMINAL UNDERWORLD.
IT'S NOT LIKE THE OLD DAYS ANYMORE.
YOU GOTTA BE DISCREET.
DING!!

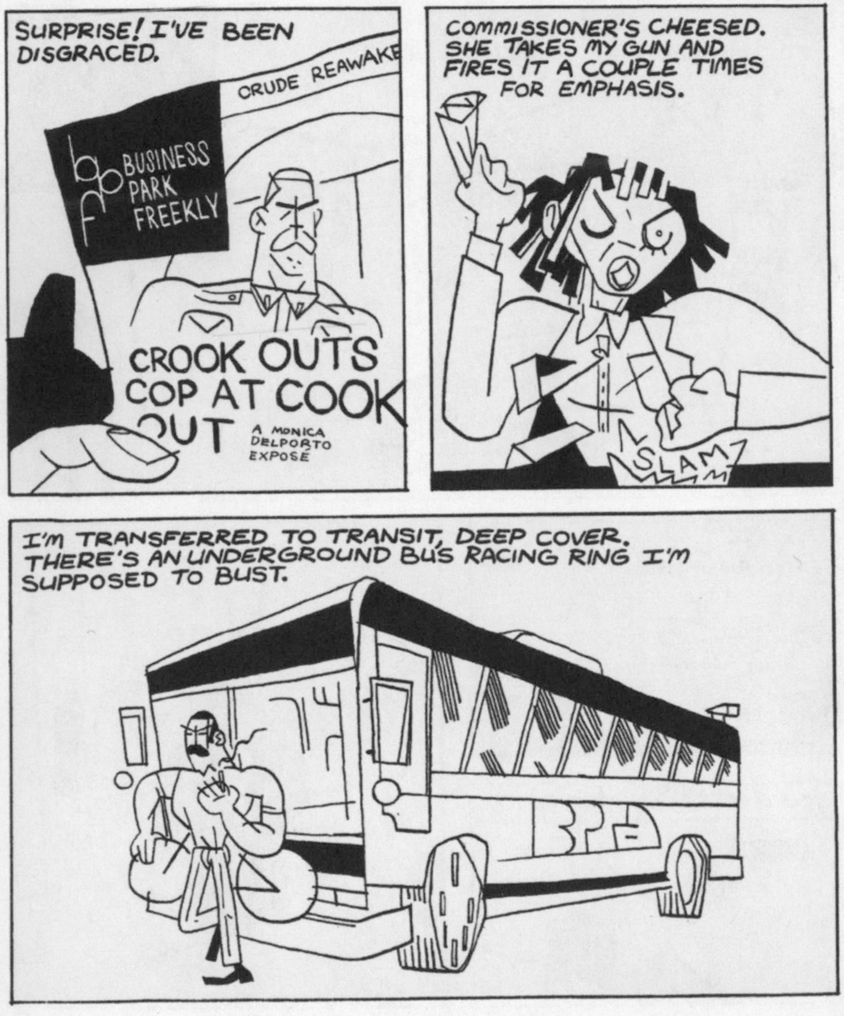
SURPRISE! I'VE BEEN DISGRACED.
CRUDE REAWAKE
BUSINESS PARK FREEKLY
CROOK OUTS COP AT COOK OUT
A MONICA DELPORTO EXPOSÉ
COMMISSIONER'S CHEESED. SHE TAKES MY GUN AND FIRES IT A COUPLE TIMES FOR EMPHASIS.
SLAM
I'M TRANSFERRED TO TRANSIT, DEEP COVER. THERE'S AN UNDERGROUND BUS RACING RING I'M SUPPOSED TO BUST.

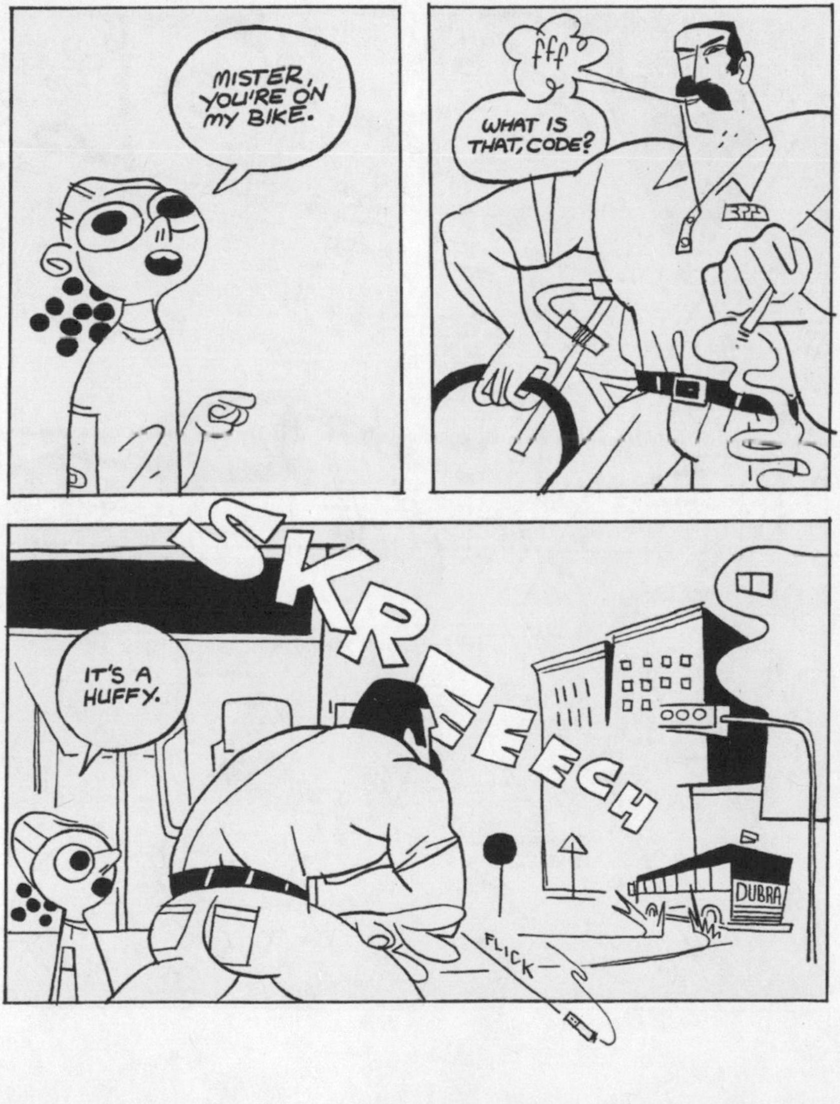
MISTER, YOU'RE ON MY BIKE.
fff
WHAT IS THAT, CODE?
SKREEECH
IT'S A HUFFY.
DUBRA
FLICK

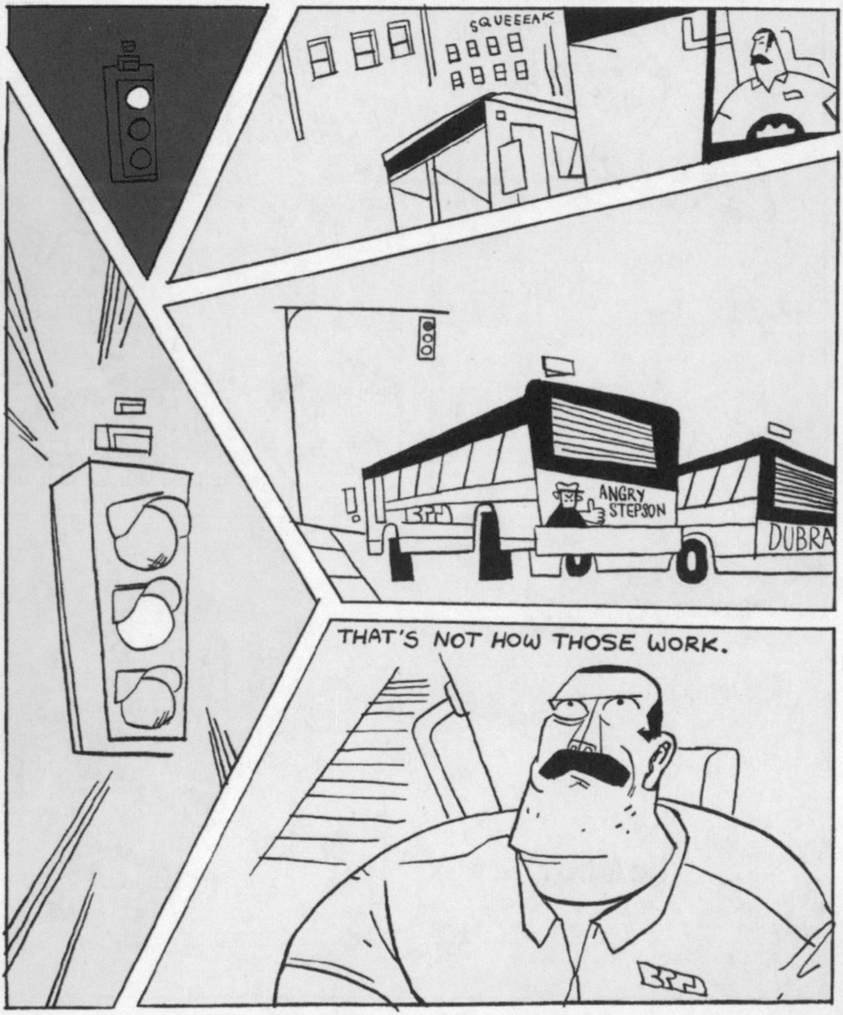
SQUEEEAK
ANGRY STEPSON
DUBRA
THAT'S NOT HOW THOSE WORK.

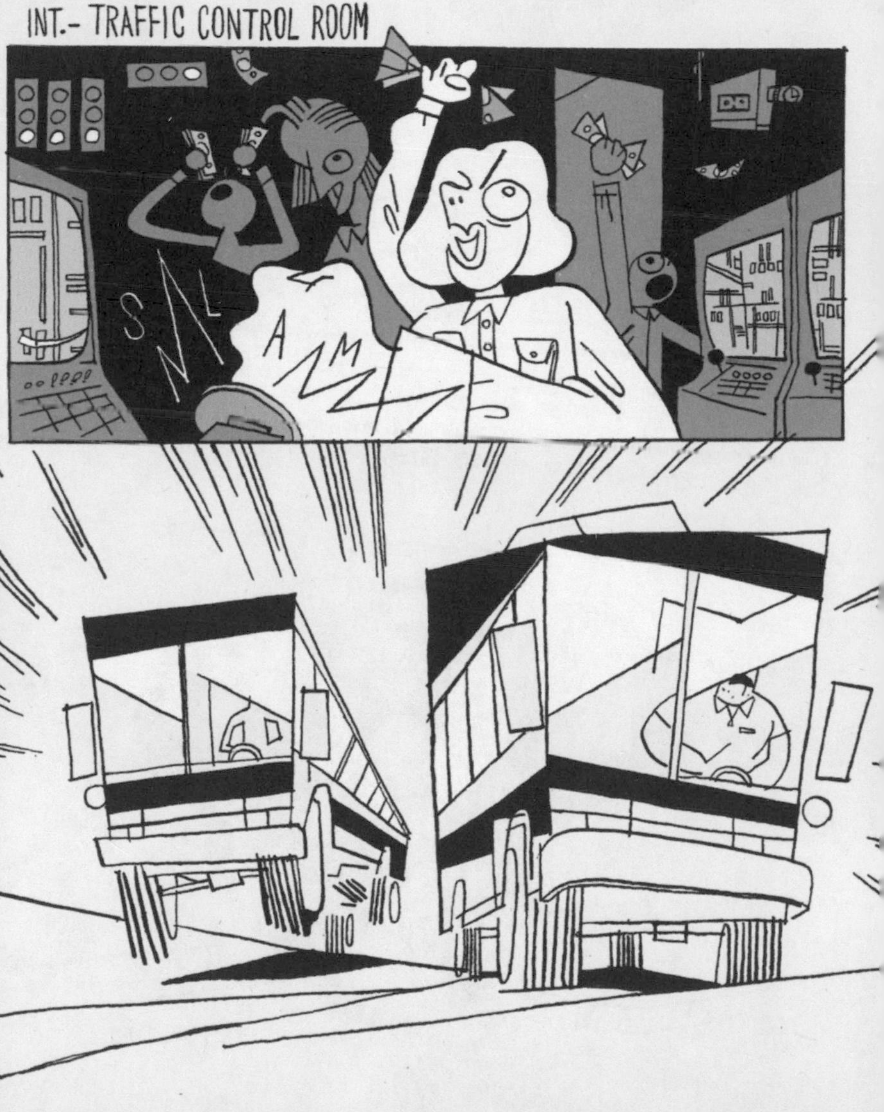
INT.- TRAFFIC CONTROL ROOM
SLAM

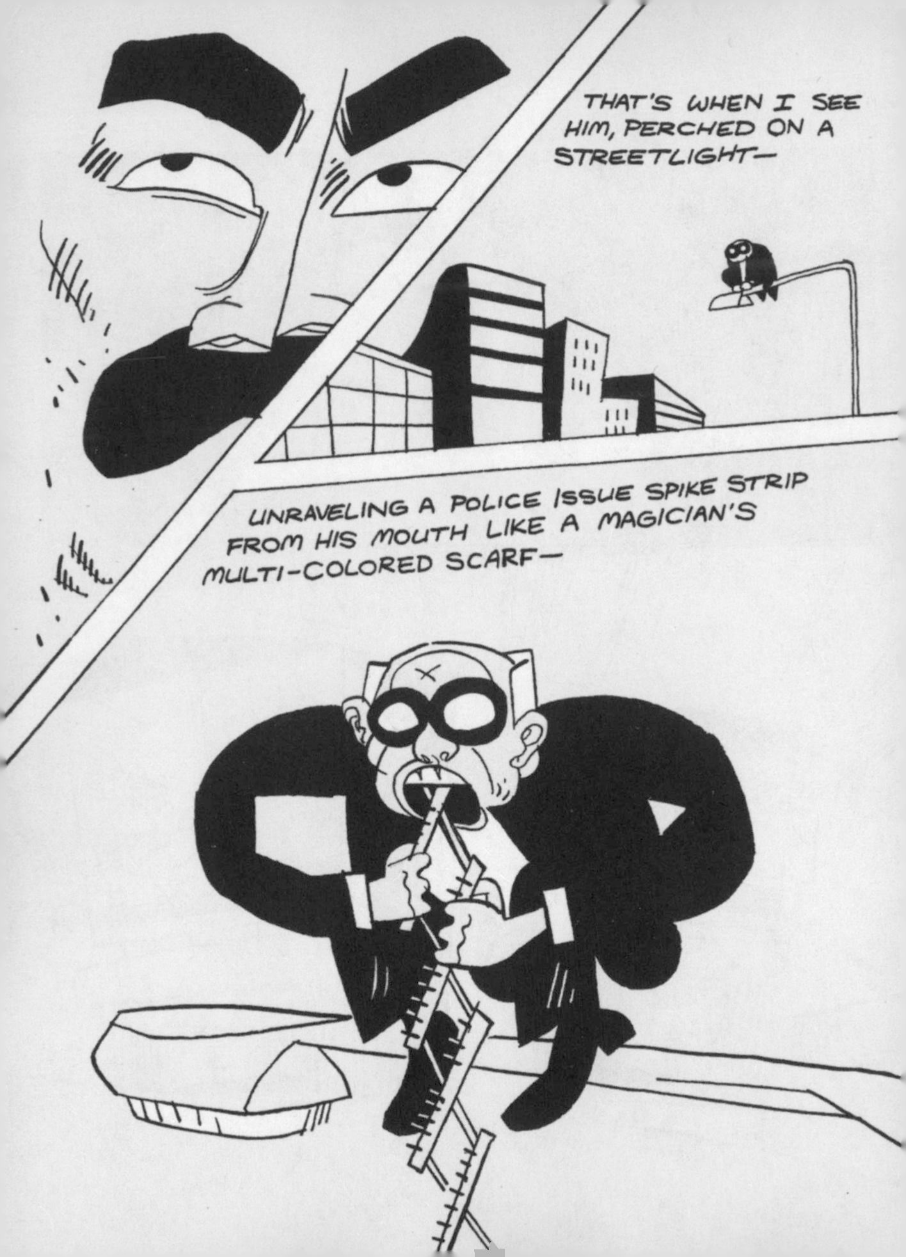
THAT'S WHEN I SEE HIM, PERCHED ON A STREETLIGHT—
UNRAVELING A POLICE ISSUE SPIKE STRIP FROM HIS MOUTH LIKE A MAGICIAN'S MULTI-COLORED SCARF—

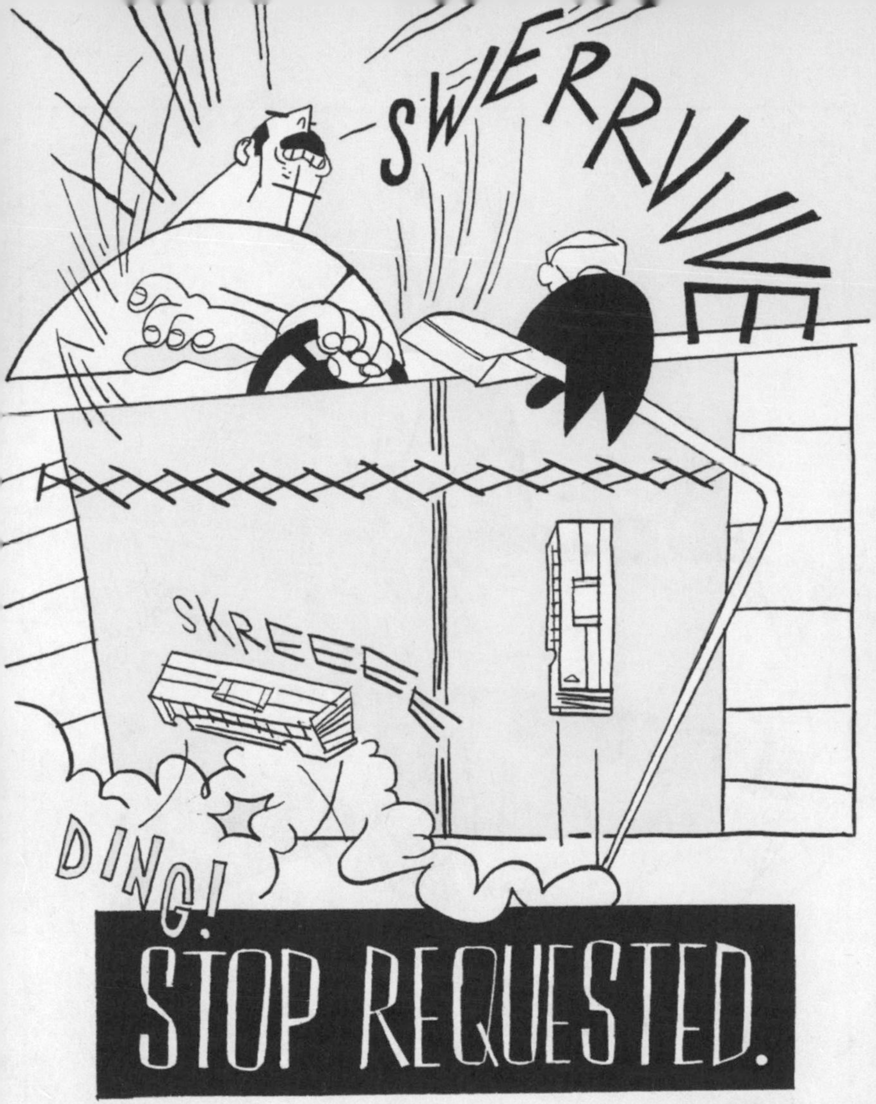
SWERRVVVE
SKREEE
DING!
STOP REQUESTED.

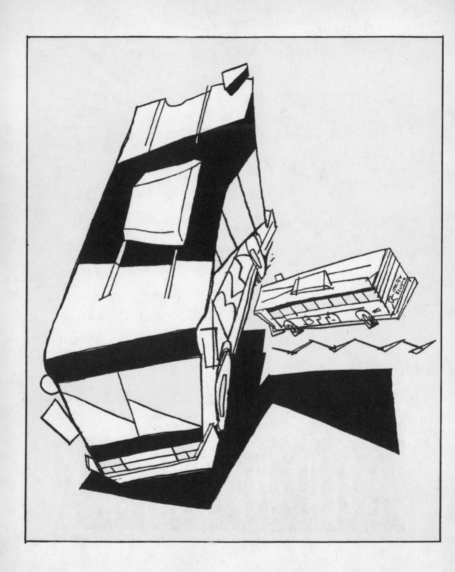

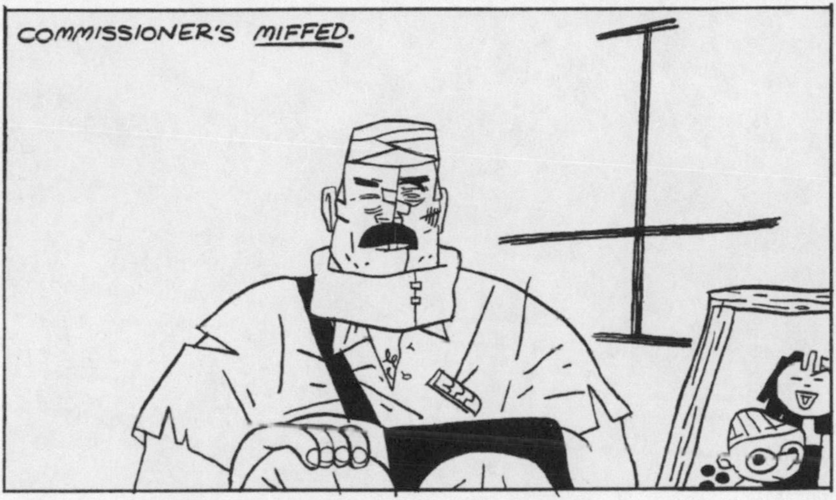
COMMISSIONER'S MIFFED.

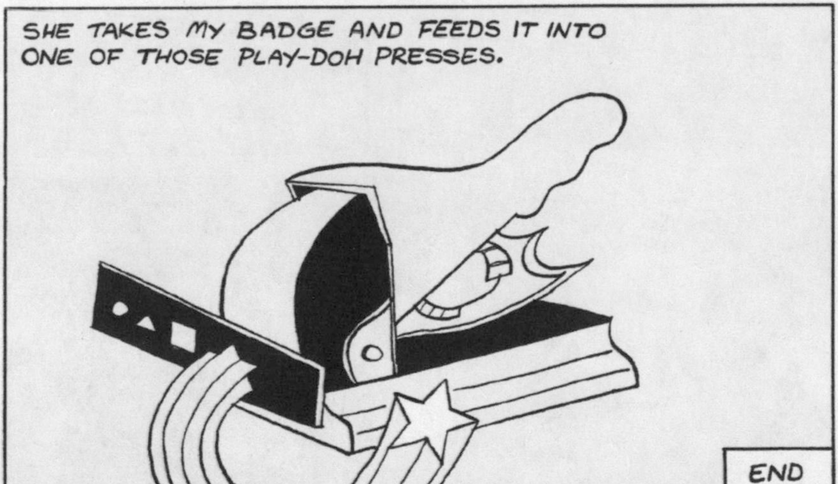
SHE TAKES MY BADGE AND FEEDS IT INTO ONE OF THOSE PLAY-DOH PRESSES.
END

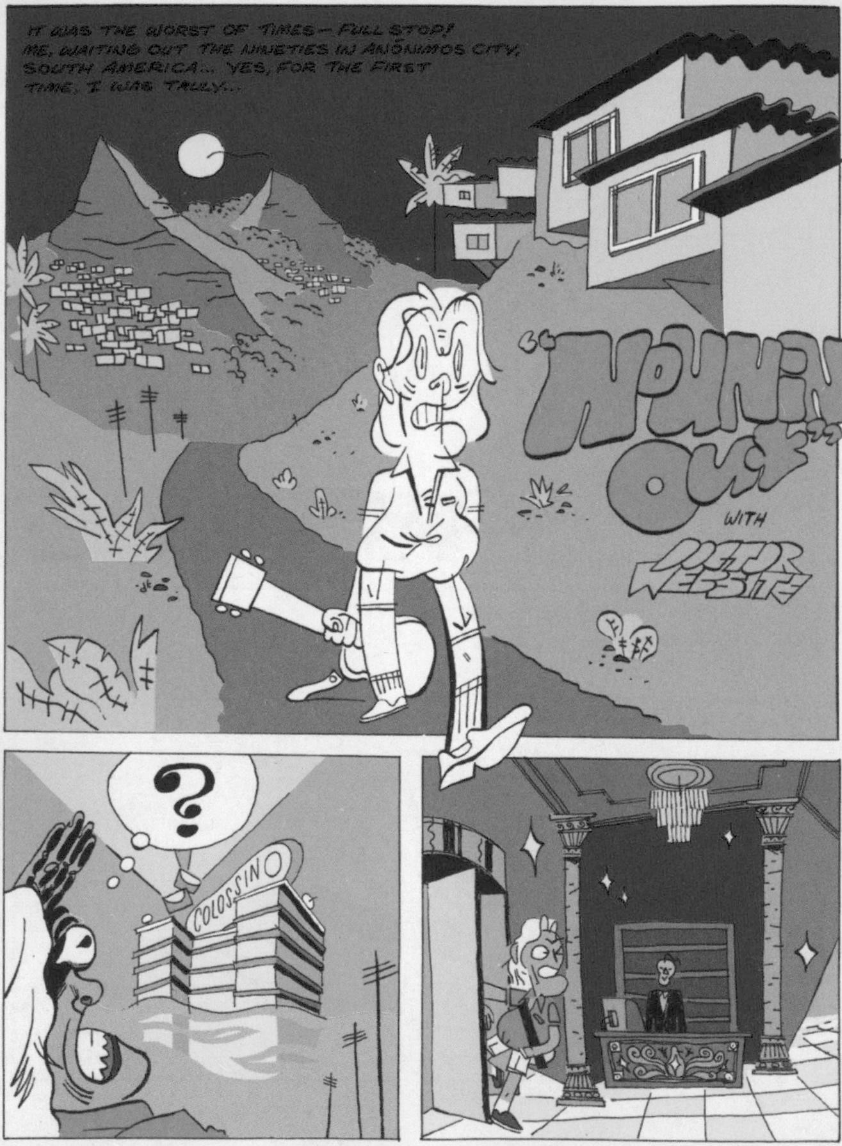
IT WAS THE WORST OF TIMES — FULL STOP!
ME, WAITING OUT THE NINETIES IN ANÓNIMOS CITY, SOUTH AMERICA... YES, FOR THE FIRST TIME, I WAS TRULY...
WITH
?
COLOSSINO

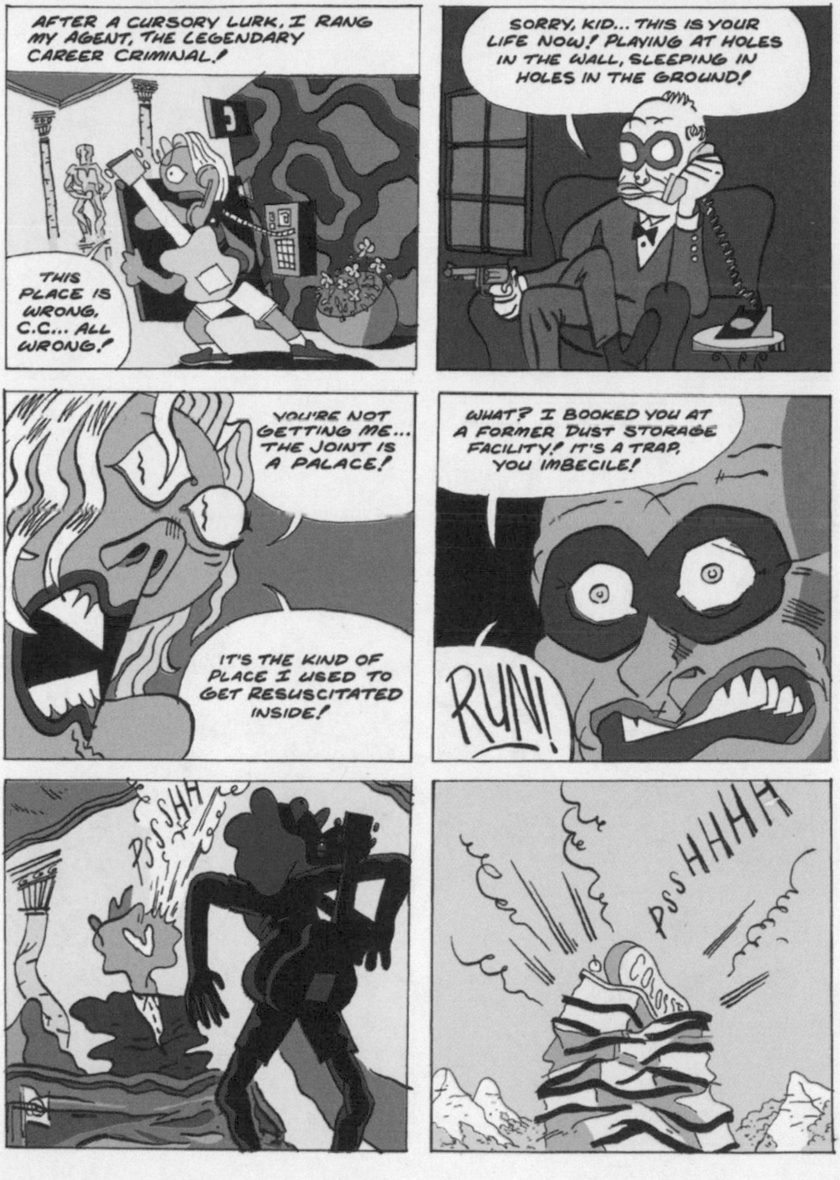
AFTER A CURSORY LURK, I RANG MY AGENT, THE LEGENDARY CAREER CRIMINAL!
THIS PLACE IS WRONG, C.C... ALL WRONG!
SORRY, KID... THIS IS YOUR LIFE NOW! PLAYING AT HOLES IN THE WALL, SLEEPING IN HOLES IN THE GROUND!
YOU'RE NOT GETTING ME... THE JOINT IS A PALACE!
IT'S THE KIND OF PLACE I USED TO GET RESUSCITATED INSIDE!
WHAT? I BOOKED YOU AT A FORMER DUST STORAGE FACILITY! IT'S A TRAP, YOU IMBECILE!
RUN!
PSSHH
PSSHHHHH
COLOSSE

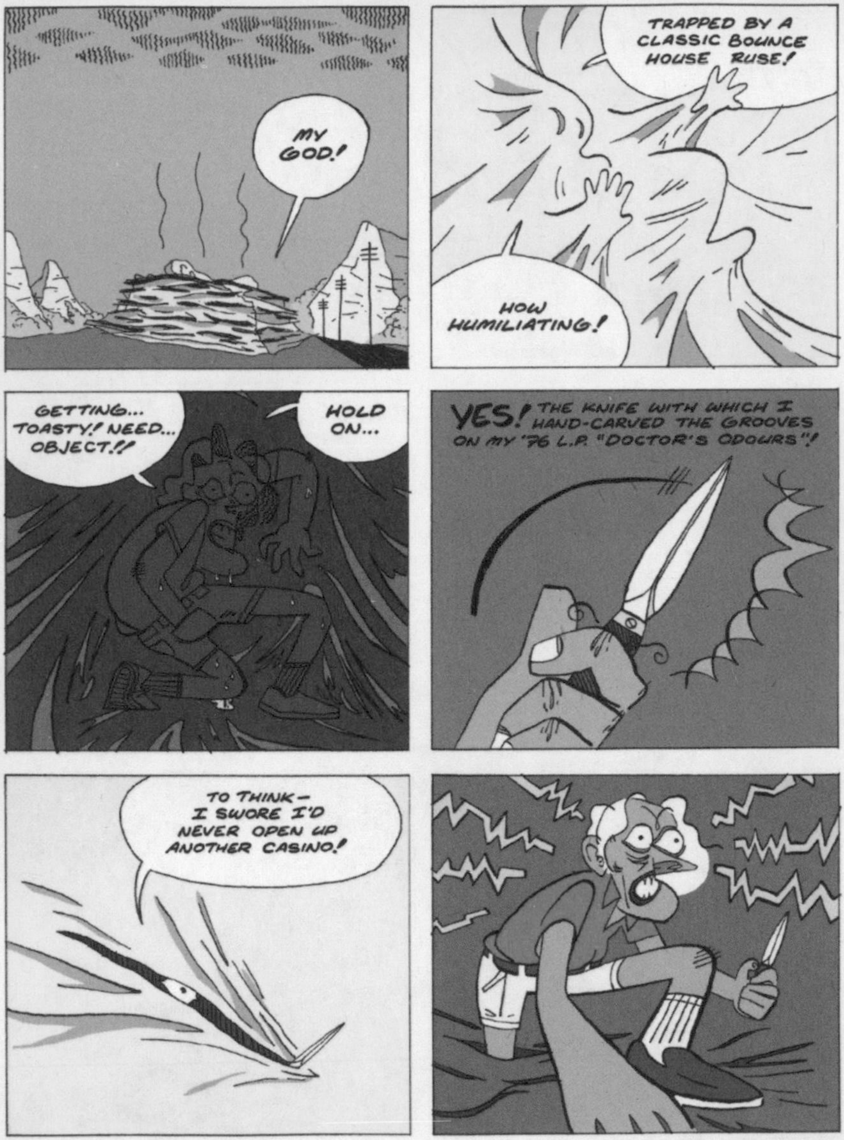
MY GOD!
TRAPPED BY A CLASSIC BOUNCE HOUSE RUSE!
HOW HUMILIATING!
GETTING... TOASTY! NEED... OBJECT.!!
HOLD ON...
YES! THE KNIFE WITH WHICH I HAND-CARVED THE GROOVES ON MY '76 L.P. "DOCTOR'S ODOURS"!
TO THINK— I SWORE I'D NEVER OPEN UP ANOTHER CASINO!

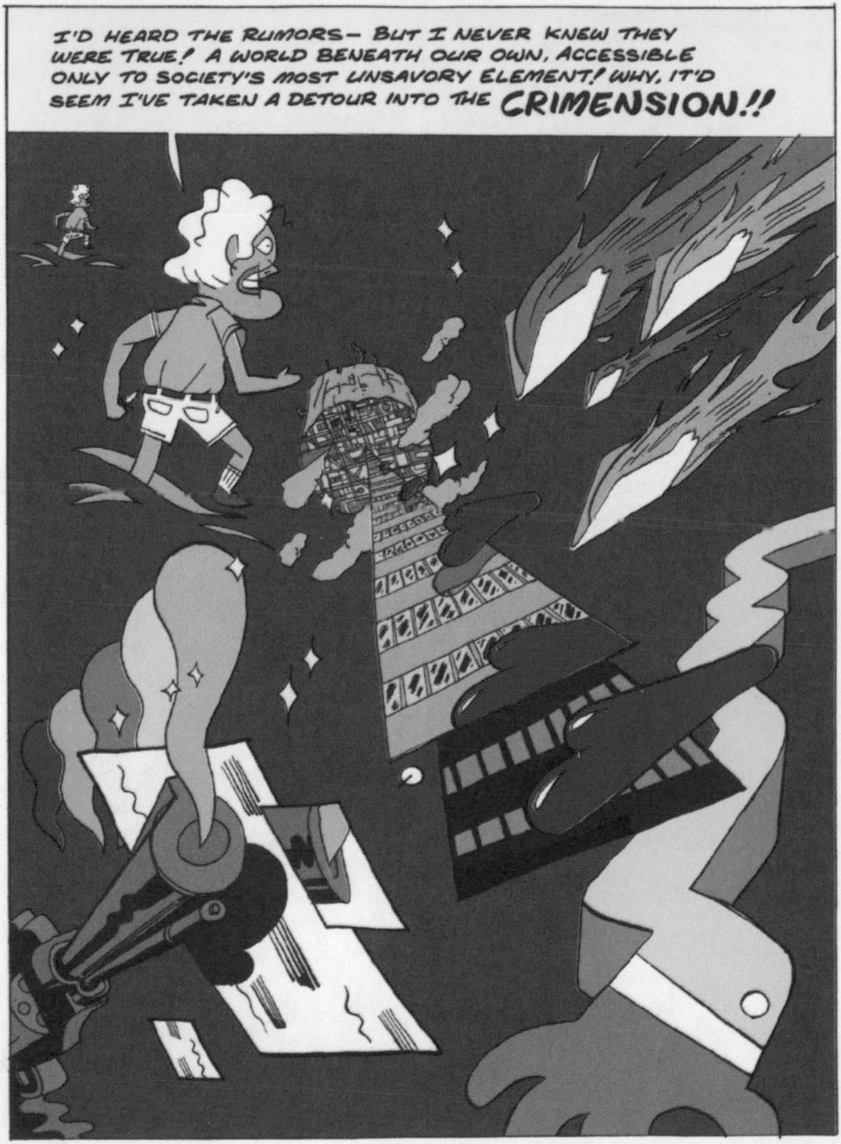
I'D HEARD THE RUMORS— BUT I NEVER KNEW THEY WERE TRUE! A WORLD BENEATH OUR OWN, ACCESSIBLE ONLY TO SOCIETY'S MOST UNSAVORY ELEMENT! WHY, IT'D SEEM I'VE TAKEN A DETOUR INTO THE CRIMENSION!!

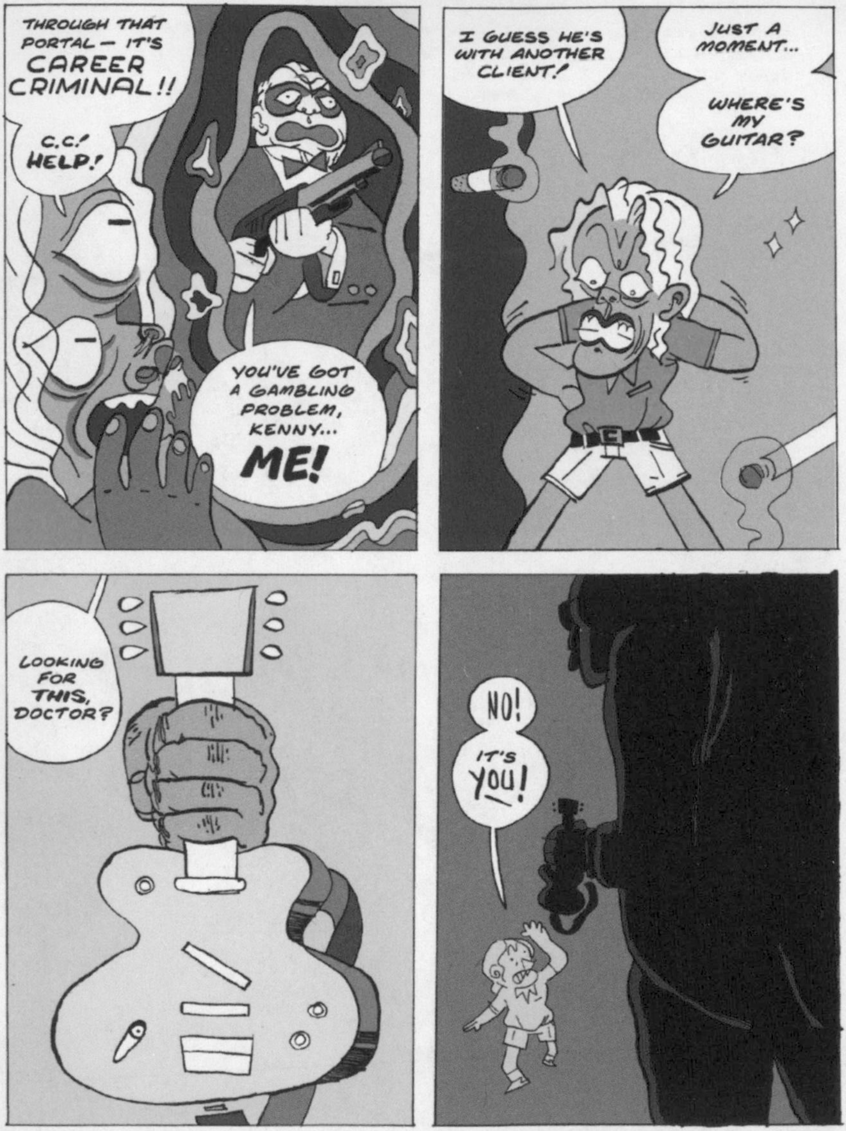
THROUGH THAT PORTAL — IT'S CAREER CRIMINAL!!
C.C.! HELP!
YOU'VE GOT A GAMBLING PROBLEM, KENNY... ME!
I GUESS HE'S WITH ANOTHER CLIENT!
JUST A MOMENT...
WHERE'S MY GUITAR?
LOOKING FOR THIS, DOCTOR?
NO!
IT'S YOU!

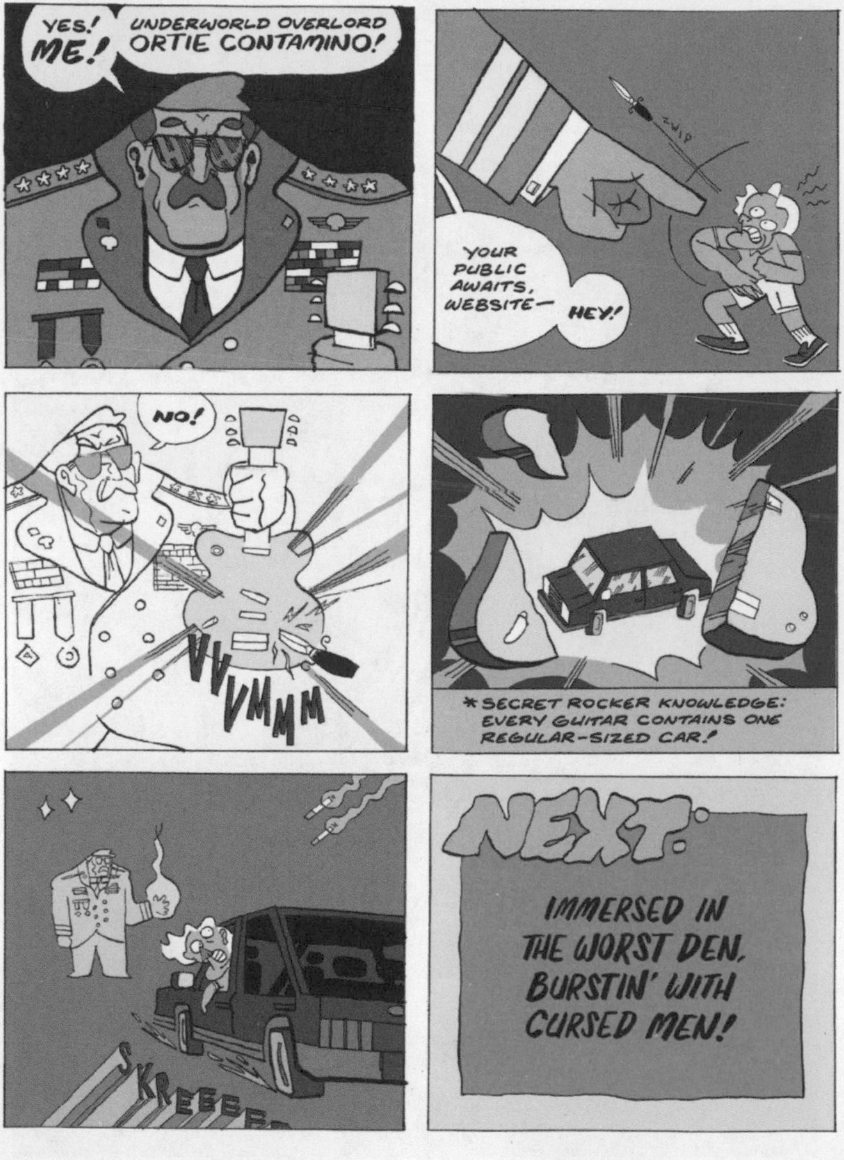

YES! ME!
UNDERWORLD OVERLORD ORTIE CONTAMINO!
ZWIP
YOUR PUBLIC AWAITS, WEBSITE—
HEY!
NO!
VVVMMM
* SECRET ROCKER KNOWLEDGE: EVERY GUITAR CONTAINS ONE REGULAR-SIZED CAR!
SKREEEE
NEXT:
IMMERSED IN THE WORST DEN, BURSTIN' WITH CURSED MEN!

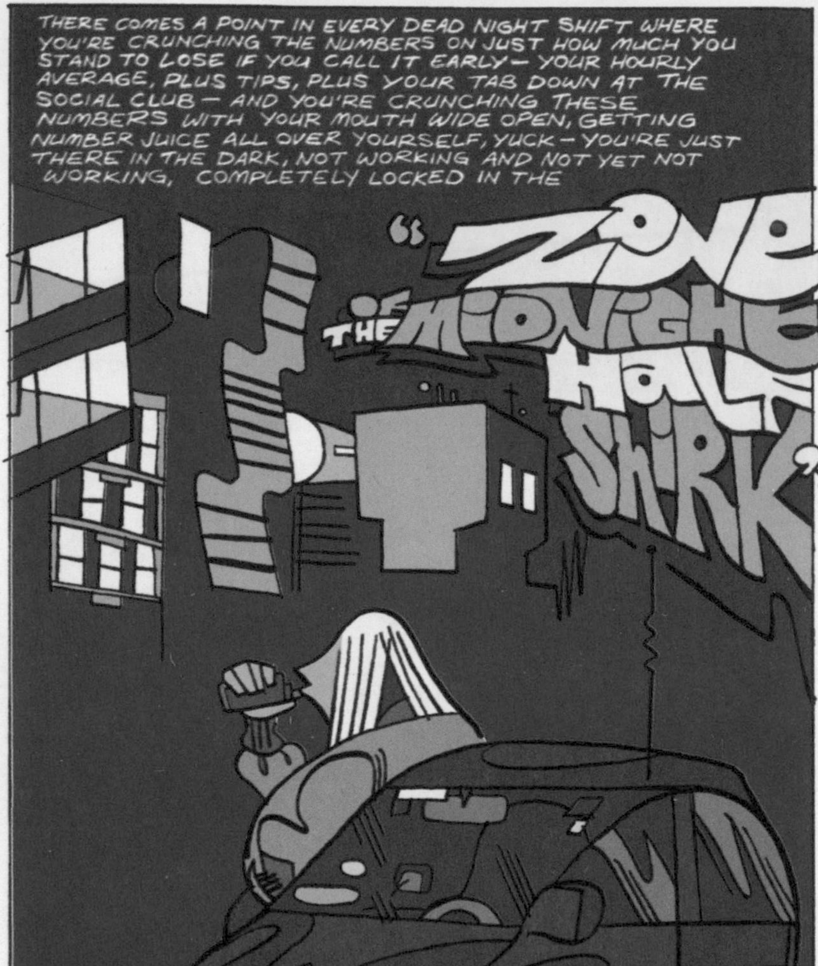
THERE COMES A POINT IN EVERY DEAD NIGHT SHIFT WHERE YOU'RE CRUNCHING THE NUMBERS ON JUST HOW MUCH YOU STAND TO LOSE IF YOU CALL IT EARLY— YOUR HOURLY AVERAGE, PLUS TIPS, PLUS YOUR TAB DOWN AT THE SOCIAL CLUB— AND YOU'RE CRUNCHING THESE NUMBERS WITH YOUR MOUTH WIDE OPEN, GETTING NUMBER JUICE ALL OVER YOURSELF, YUCK— YOU'RE JUST THERE IN THE DARK, NOT WORKING AND NOT YET NOT WORKING, COMPLETELY LOCKED IN THE
"ZONE OF THE MIDNIGHT HALF SHIRK"

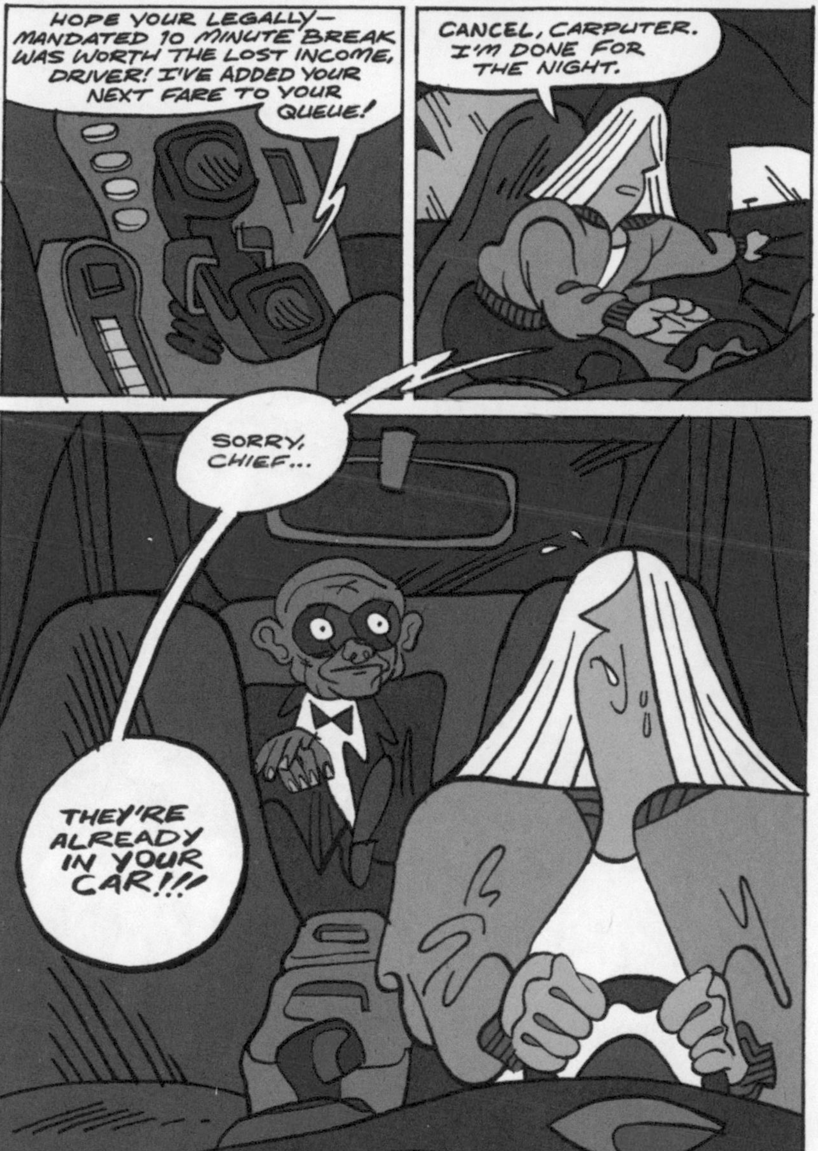
HOPE YOUR LEGALLY-MANDATED 10 MINUTE BREAK WAS WORTH THE LOST INCOME, DRIVER! I'VE ADDED YOUR NEXT FARE TO YOUR QUEUE!
CANCEL, CARPUTER. I'M DONE FOR THE NIGHT.
SORRY, CHIEF...
THEY'RE ALREADY IN YOUR CAR!!!

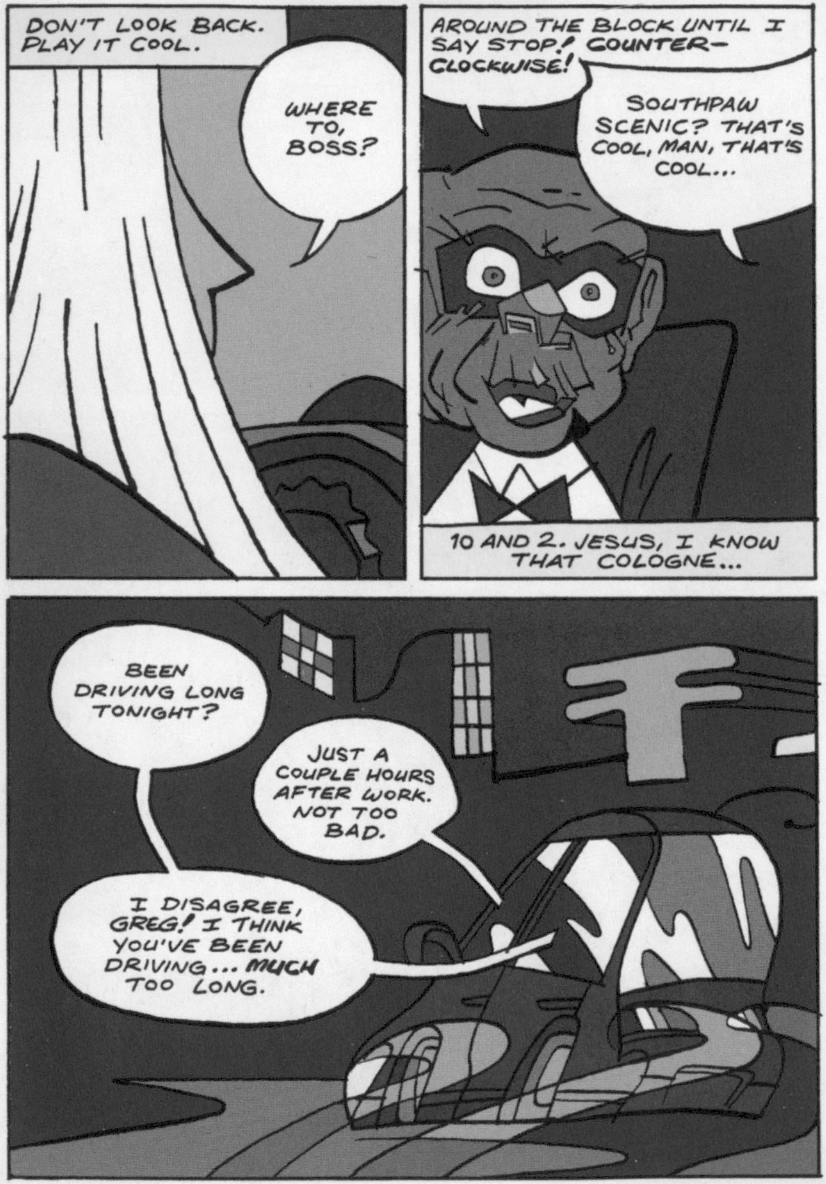
DON'T LOOK BACK. PLAY IT COOL.
WHERE TO, BOSS?
AROUND THE BLOCK UNTIL I SAY STOP! COUNTER-CLOCKWISE!
SOUTHPAW SCENIC? THAT'S COOL, MAN, THAT'S COOL...
10 AND 2. JESUS, I KNOW THAT COLOGNE...
BEEN DRIVING LONG TONIGHT?
JUST A COUPLE HOURS AFTER WORK. NOT TOO BAD.
I DISAGREE, GREG! I THINK YOU'VE BEEN DRIVING... MUCH TOO LONG.

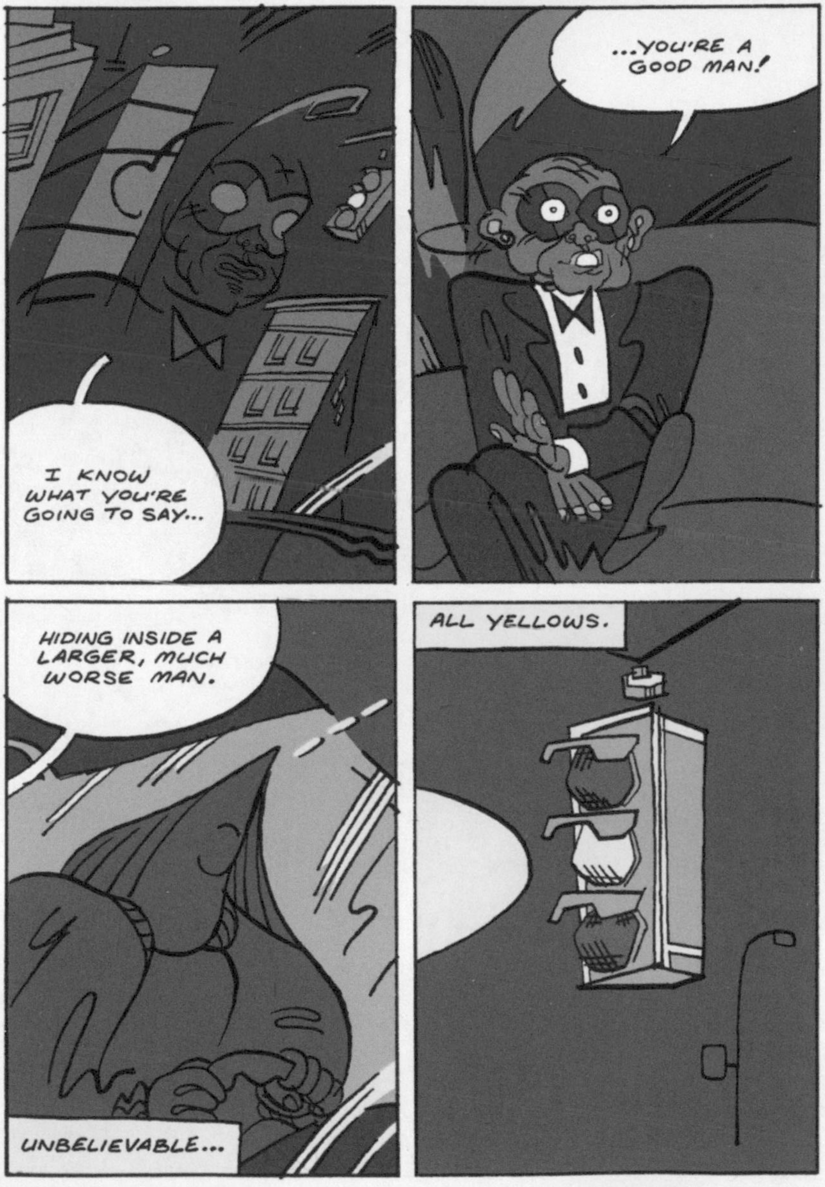
I KNOW WHAT YOU'RE GOING TO SAY...
...YOU'RE A GOOD MAN!
HIDING INSIDE A LARGER, MUCH WORSE MAN.
UNBELIEVABLE...
ALL YELLOWS.

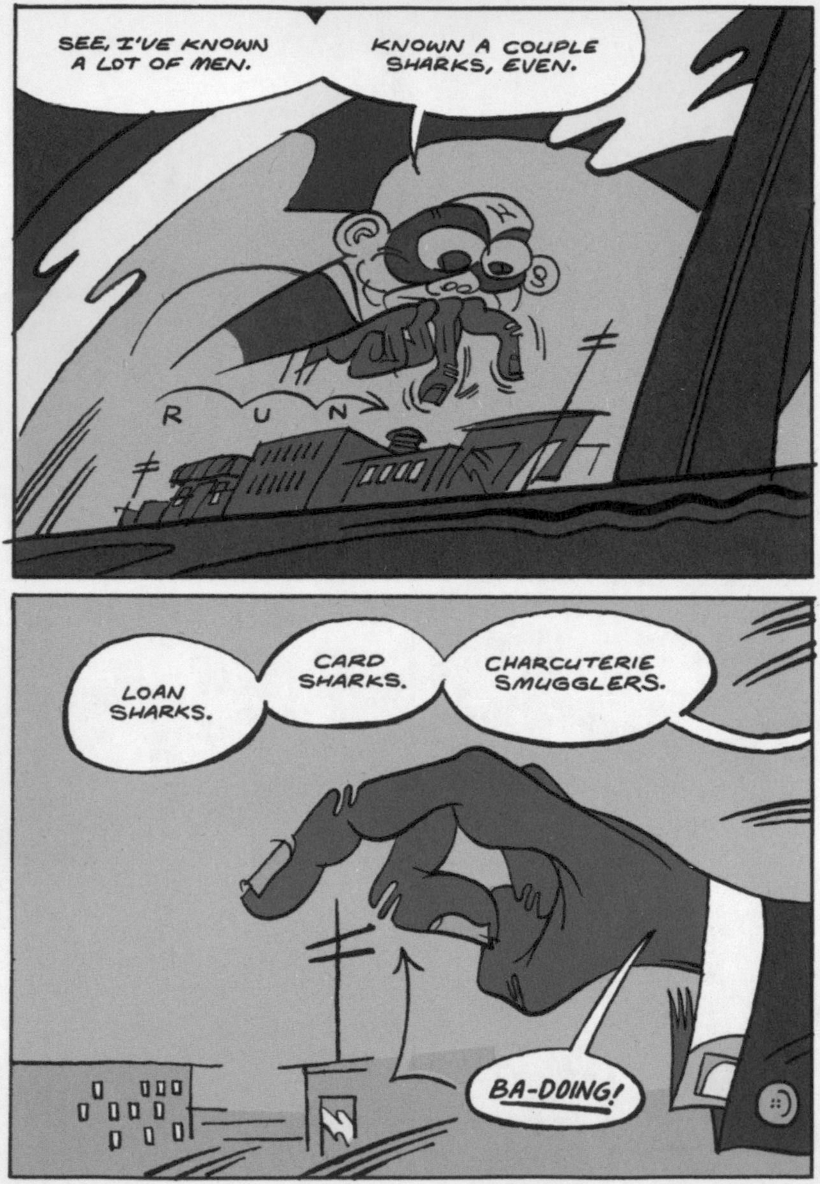
SEE, I'VE KNOWN A LOT OF MEN.
KNOWN A COUPLE SHARKS, EVEN.
R U N
LOAN SHARKS.
CARD SHARKS.
CHARCUTERIE SMUGGLERS.
BA-DOING!

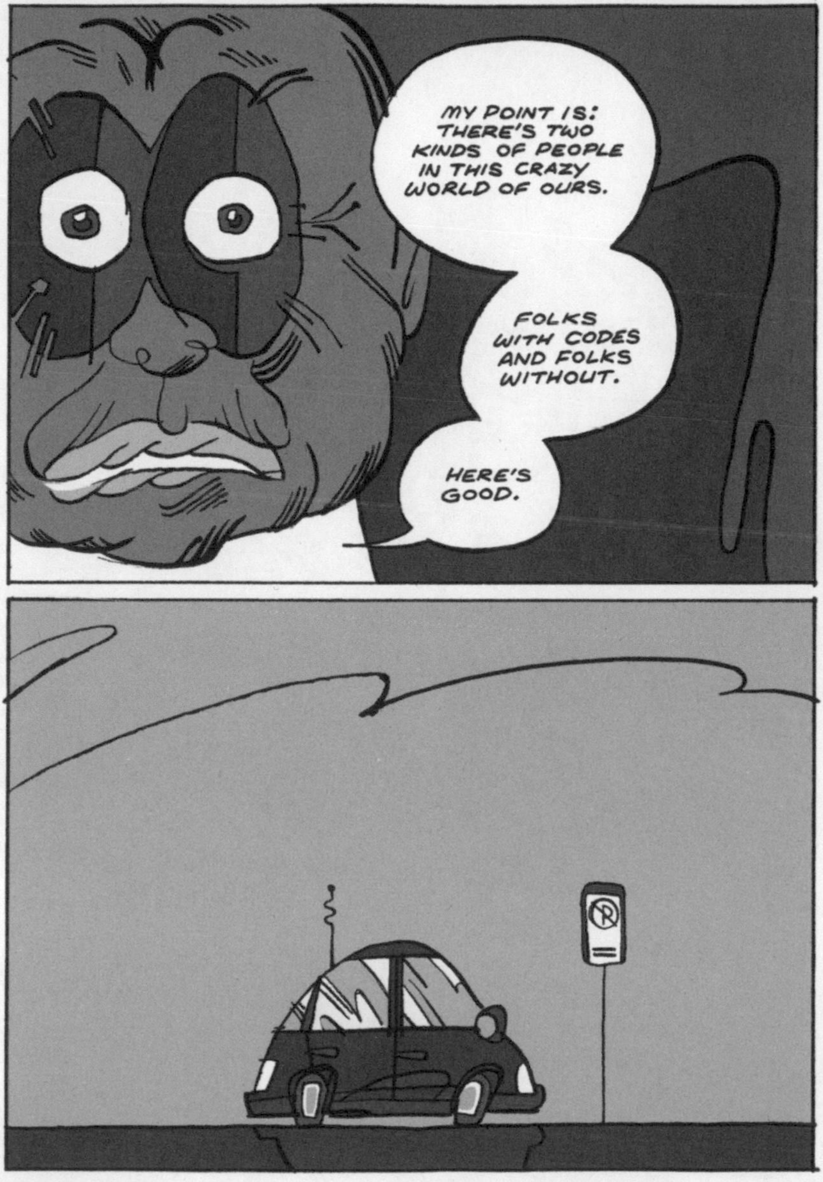
MY POINT IS: THERE'S TWO KINDS OF PEOPLE IN THIS CRAZY WORLD OF OURS.
FOLKS WITH CODES AND FOLKS WITHOUT.
HERE'S GOOD.

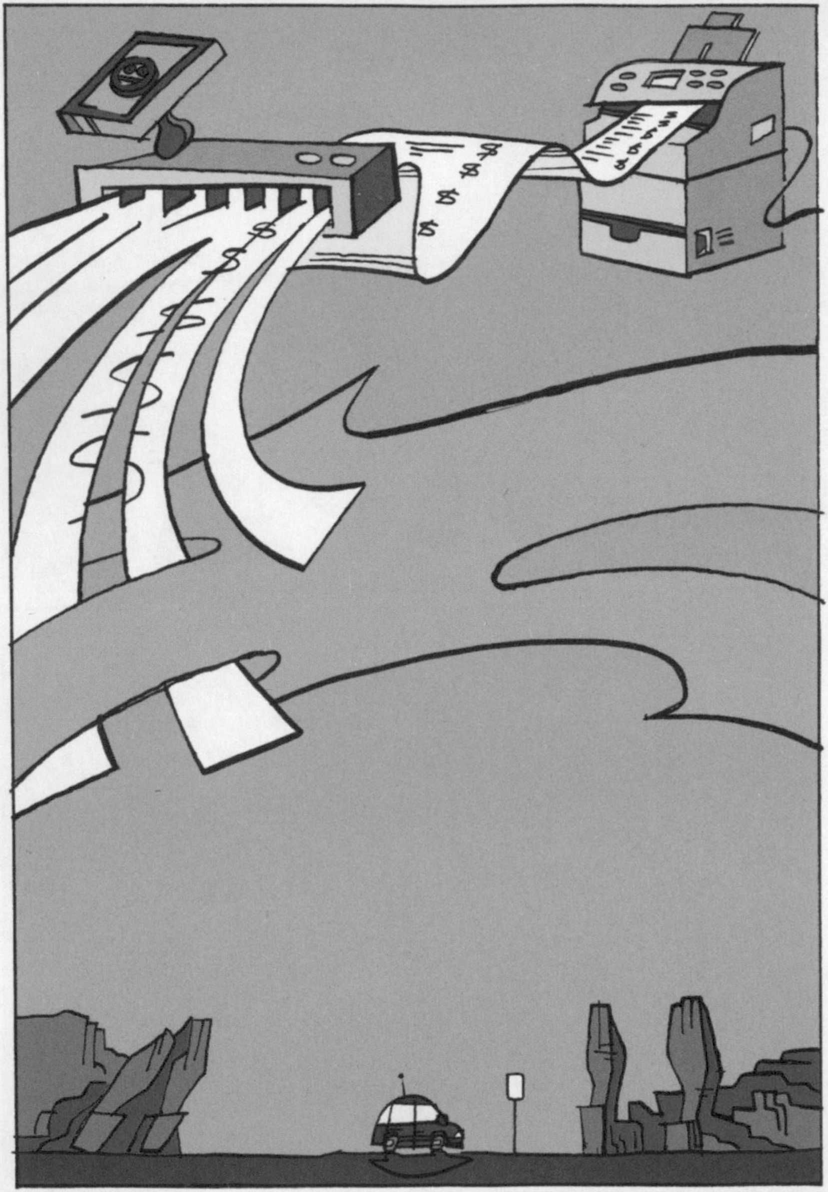

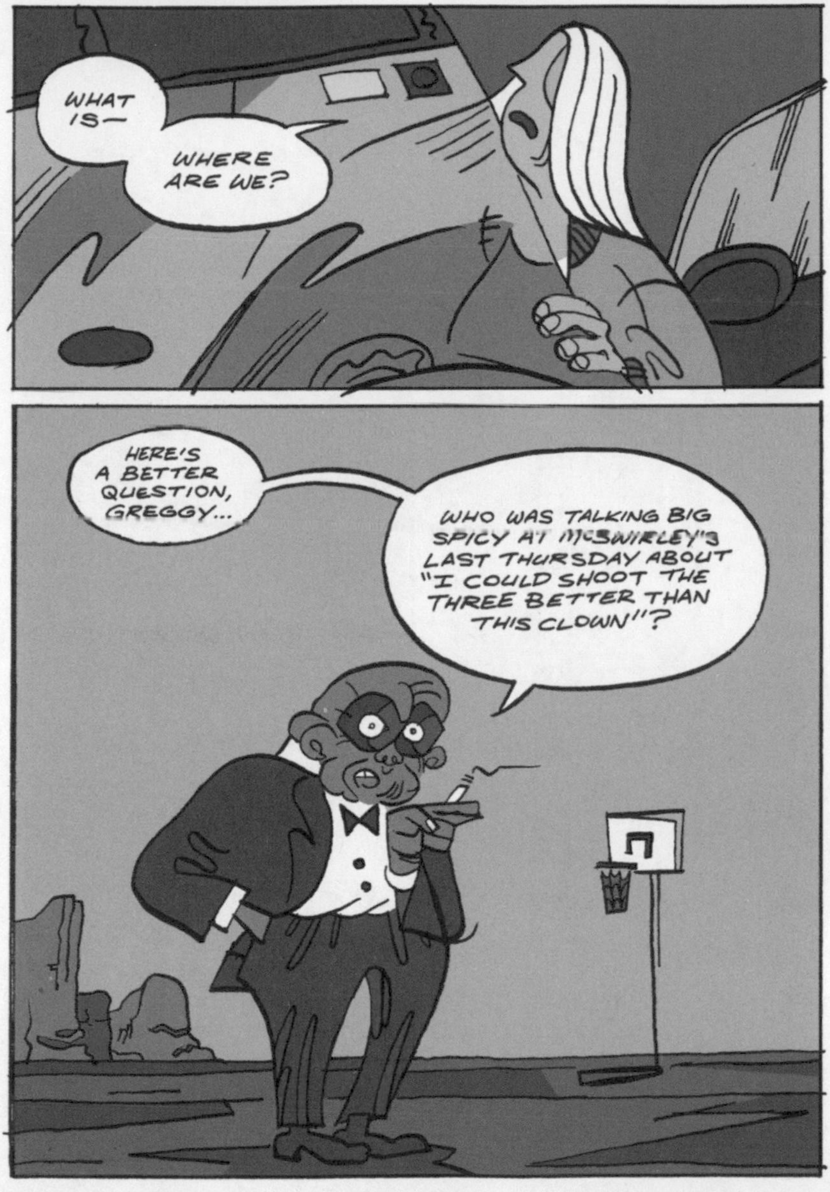
WHAT IS—
WHERE ARE WE?
HERE'S A BETTER QUESTION, GREGGY...
WHO WAS TALKING BIG SPICY AT McSWIRLEY'S LAST THURSDAY ABOUT "I COULD SHOOT THE THREE BETTER THAN THIS CLOWN"?

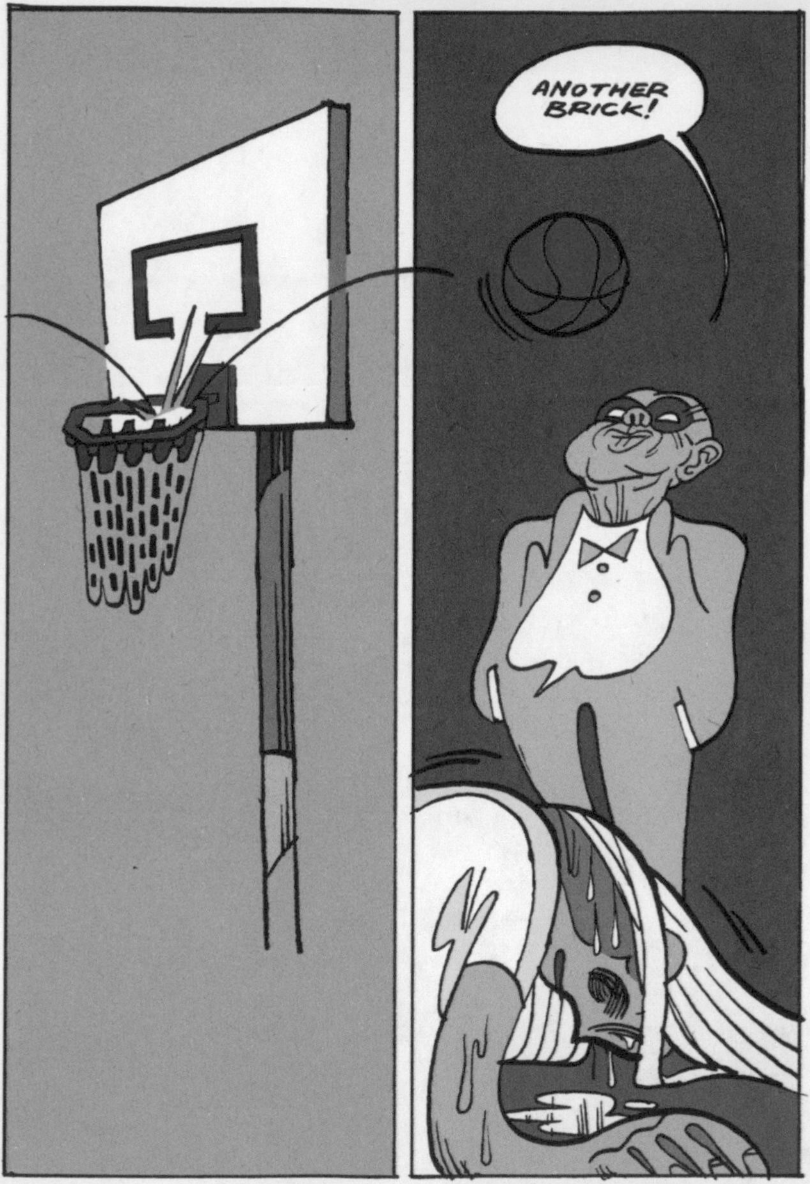
ANOTHER BRICK!

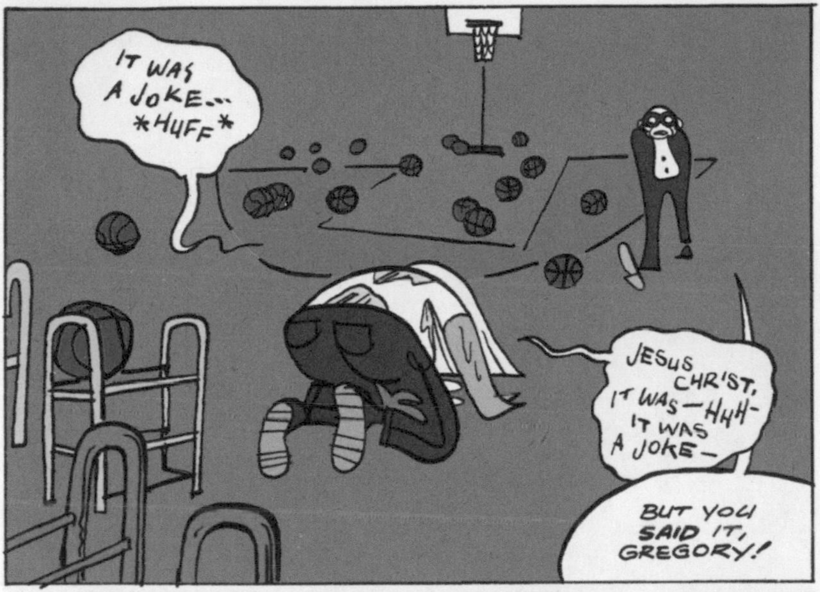
IT WAS A JOKE... *HUFF*
JESUS CHRIST, IT WAS—HHH— IT WAS A JOKE—
BUT YOU SAID IT, GREGORY!

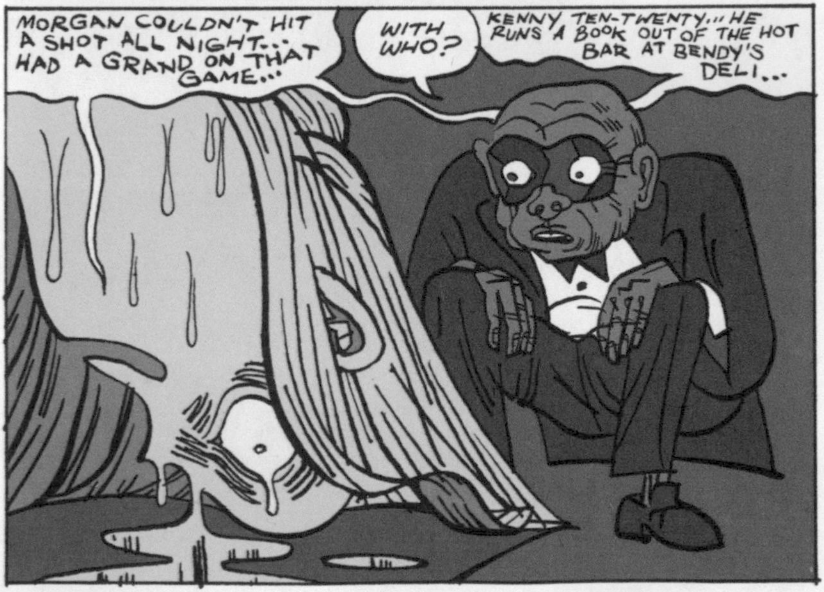
MORGAN COULDN'T HIT A SHOT ALL NIGHT... HAD A GRAND ON THAT GAME...
WITH WHO?
KENNY TEN-TWENTY... HE RUNS A BOOK OUT OF THE HOT BAR AT BENDY'S DELI...

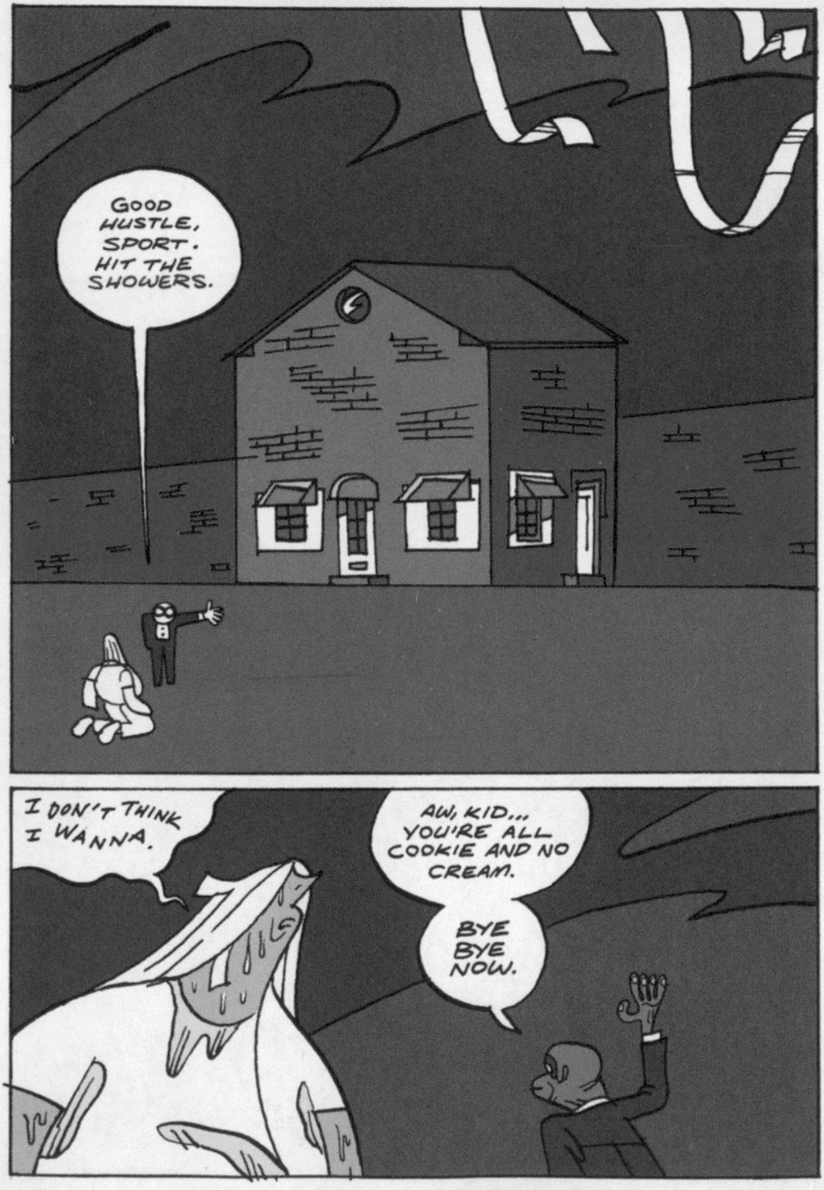
GOOD HUSTLE, SPORT. HIT THE SHOWERS.
I DON'T THINK I WANNA.
AW, KID... YOU'RE ALL COOKIE AND NO CREAM.
BYE BYE NOW.

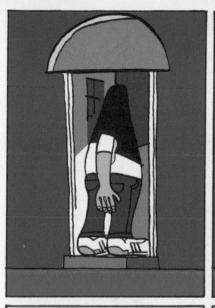

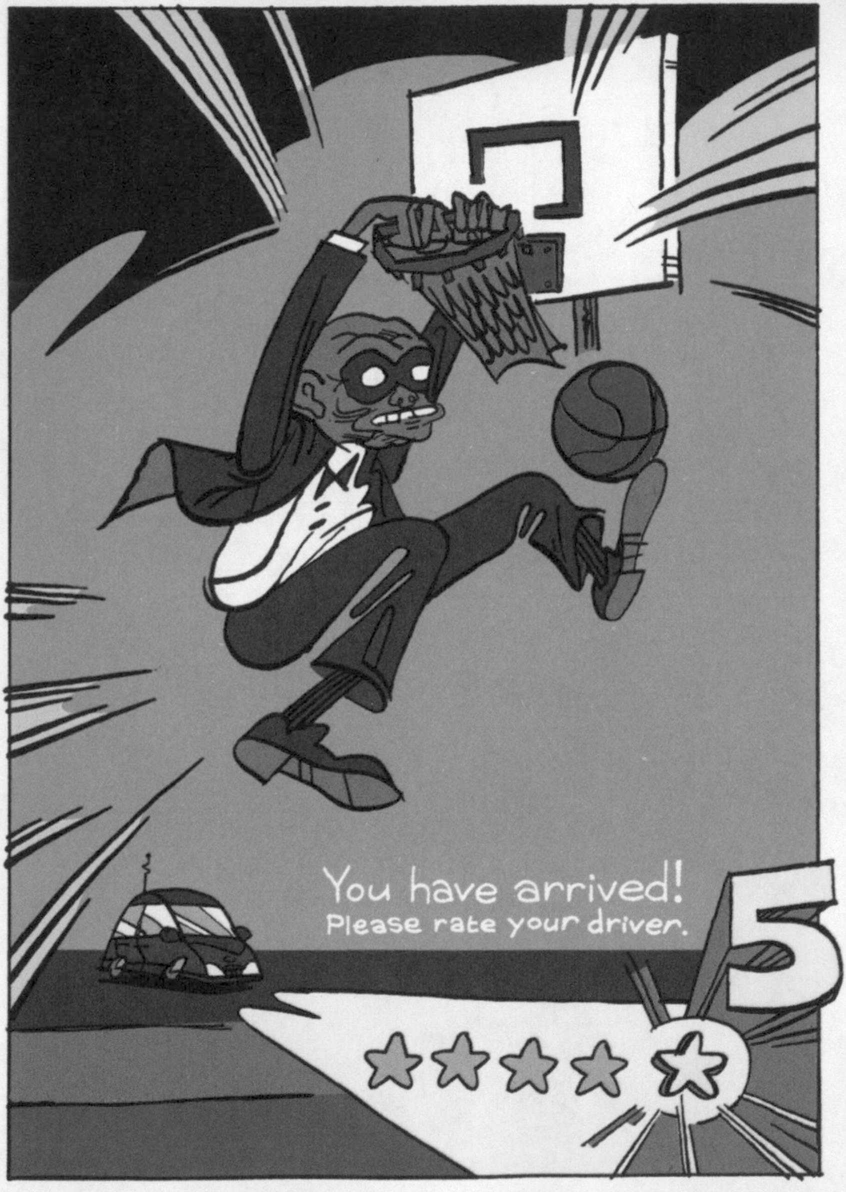
You have arrived!
Please rate your driver.
5

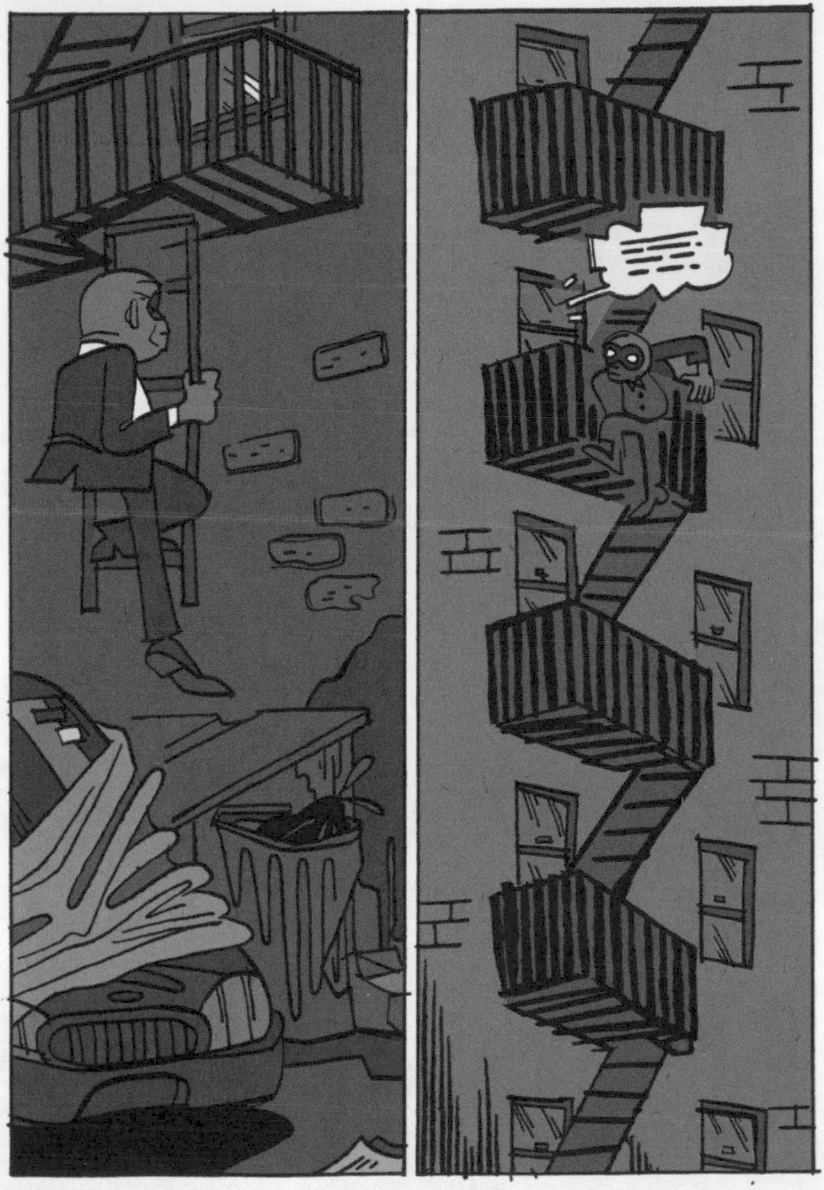

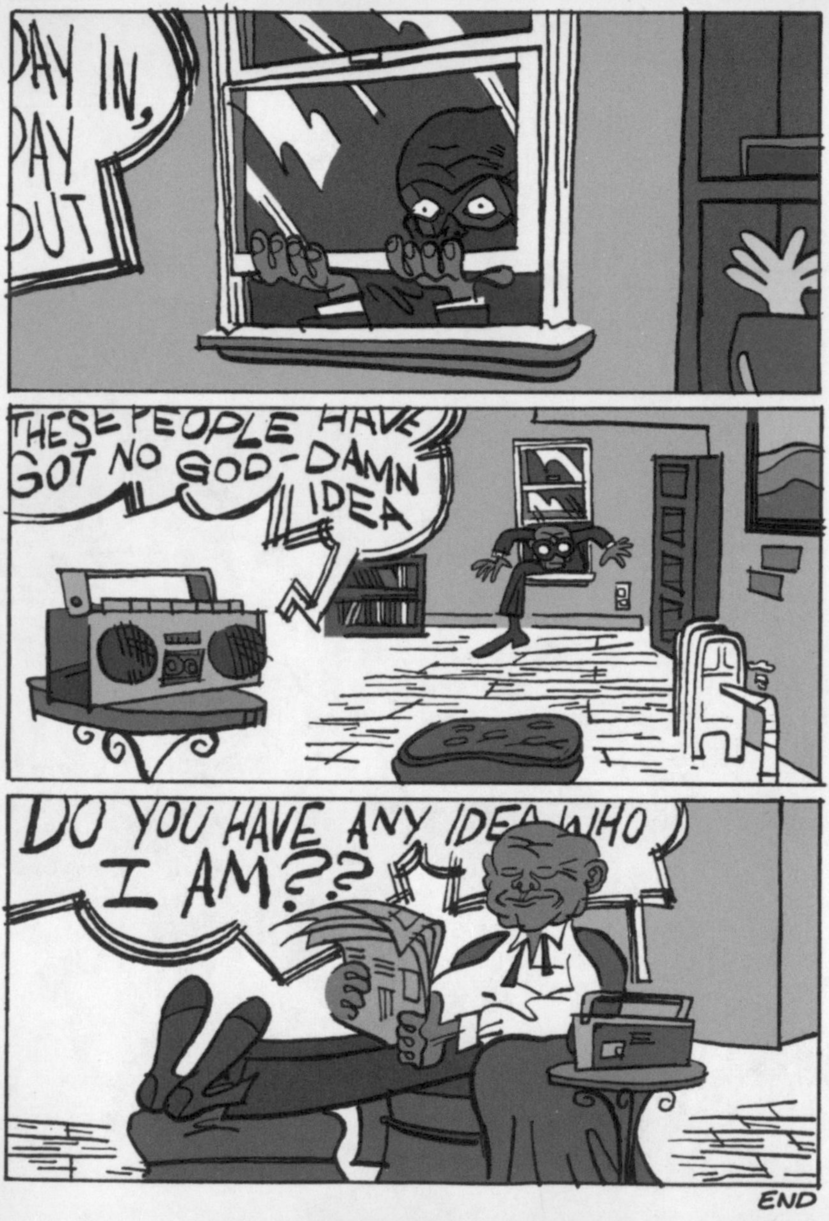
DAY IN, DAY OUT
THESE PEOPLE HAVE GOT NO GOD-DAMN IDEA
DO YOU HAVE ANY IDEA WHO I AM??
END

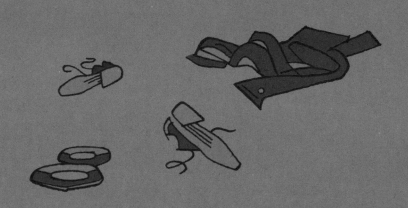

"LOOKS LIKE THIS GUY GOT HIMSELF A LIFETIME SUBSCRIPTION TO _FUCKED UP & DEAD WEEKLY_... AND IT JUST EXPIRED."

"YUP... THAT'S BLOOD."

NOTES

TENNELL LEFFITT MAN DETECTIVE
WAS ORIGINALLY WRITTEN IN 2015 AND
HAS BEEN REDRAWN FOR THIS COLLECTION.
TRIP SPLAIN WAS PRINTED IN THE MINICOMIC
GARAGE ISLAND #4 IN 2017. NOUNIN OUT
FIRST APPEARED IN THE XTRA LARGE WEAKLY
ANNUAL IN 2016 AND HAS BEEN RELETTERED.